FAITH &
Optimism

Positive Expectation in the Christian Life

M. Blaine Smith

SilverC
B•O•O•

I

Why Be Optimistic?

1

A Well-Founded Choice

Recently a friend of mine, Jennifer, reached an impasse in a relationship. She has dated Brad for over two years, with the hope of eventually marrying him. Yet they had a serious talk, and Brad conceded that even though they are both in their mid-thirties, he isn't ready yet for a lifetime commitment. While he didn't rule out the possibility at some future point, he knew he wasn't ready for marriage at this time.

Although Brad's response was far from a full-scale rejection, it flew like a mountain of sand in the face of Jennifer's expectations for the relationship and seemed to her like a death sentence. Worst of all, she felt cursed by the heavens. "I just don't understand the hand of God in this," she complained. "I've never been in a relationship where I've tried more diligently to honor God and follow his principles. And it seems that God has given me so many reasons for hope during the time I've dated Brad. But now it appears he has simply set me up to shoot me down. I just don't believe that God has dealt fairly with me."

Jennifer's feelings of discouragement are only too understand-able. Disappointments in relationships are among the most painful experiences we suffer. There are few of us who wouldn't feel de-jected in similar circumstances. Yet her hurt was intensified by the conclusions she reached about God's role in what happened. She read these circumstances to mean that God had turned against her; worse still, he was treating her unjustly.

I talk with many Christians who have fallen into an outlook similar to Jennifer's. They've concluded that God is unconcerned with helping them, even that he wishes to punish and harm them. Sometimes such thinking is merely temporary—part of the cathar-sis of coming to terms with a personal loss. Yet all too frequently it becomes an abiding way of interpreting what God is doing in their experience.

The tragedy is that when we conclude that God isn't treating us fairly in one situation, it's only a small jump to thinking he cannot be trusted with anything else. Optimism about our future fades, and we lose the courage to take steps of faith. I find this to be the state of affairs with numerous Christians today, even some with consid-erable doctrinal understanding. When it comes to considering the role of God in their lives, they get locked into pessimism.

Half-Empty or Half-Full?

There are exceptions, though, and some truly inspiring ones at that. Consider the experience another friend, Nelson, recently shared with me.

As Nelson was pulling into a parking space at his office in Wash-ington, D.C., a rear tire dropped off his car. Just one week before, while he was visiting his family in Illinois, an auto clinic had over-hauled the axle. Now Nelson faced the unhappy prospect of has-sling with a repair facility six hundred miles away which had done shoddy work—and the likelihood of another costly repair here in Washington. Not to mention the aggravation and expense of find-ing transportation in the interim, since he was bereft of his only car.

Nelson's instinctive reaction was not anger but awe. "I was astounded to think that I had driven all the way from Illinois with a faulty axle and nothing happened," he said. "If it had snapped at high speed on an interstate, I could have been killed." He then added, almost as an afterthought, that he found it impossible to feel much anxiety over how he would afford another major repair. "The same God who protected my life in this incident will provide the money needed to fix my car," he explained.

Both Jennifer and Nelson experienced significant personal setbacks which led them to reflect about God's purpose in what had happened. But while Jennifer concluded that God had turned against her, Nelson assumed God had done him a favor. Their conclusions could hardly have been farther apart.

I should hasten to say that I do not condemn Jennifer for her reaction. She is making the effort to think things through from the standpoint of her relationship with Christ, and I admire her honesty. She is a new Christian, and with her openness to expressing honestly what she is thinking and feeling, she may well work things through to a more positive perspective.

Yet while I respect Jennifer's way of thinking, I *envy* Nelson's. His is the sort of intensely hopeful outlook which I long to have characterize my own life and wish to hold out as a role model to others.

One reason I envy Nelson's manner of thinking is that I know the benefits this sort of mindset brings. When we're viewing God's work in our lives optimistically, we feel encouraged; our anxieties are lifted, we regain a sense of hope, we start seeing hidden serendipities in otherwise frustrating circumstances. Often, too, we see solutions to problems that seem insurmountable when we're thinking less optimistically.

The effects of this optimism spill over into many areas of our lives. Nelson's experience with the car has even had a positive effect on the way he looks at relationships. Though he recently went through a difficult breakup, he is viewing the situation positively that we become righteous before God (Rom 3:22; Phil 3:9), enjoy a personal relationship with Christ (Eph 3:17), are enabled to pray effectively (Eph 3:12) and become able to understand otherwise puzzling matters of doctrine (Heb 11:3). We experience God's protection through faith (1 Pet 1:5) and put ourselves in position to enjoy all of the other benefits that he extends to us (Gal 3:22; Heb 6:12). Indeed, the writer of Hebrews states it most inclusively in saying, "Without faith it is impossible to please God" (Heb 11:6).

Given the extraordinary extent to which Scripture extols faith and our need for it, it is important for us as Christians to give close and frequent attention to what an attitude of faith is and to whether our life is reflecting it. Far too often our instinctive reaction to challenges is like Jennifer's rather than Nelson's. We each have an ongoing, chronic and desperate need for the rekindling of our faith and for experiencing the optimism which faith inspires.

Where We're Heading

My hope in writing this book is to make a contribution to that process. One thing I want to do is consider specifically what a perspective of faith involves. In the next chapter we will consider four outlooks which are central to the biblical attitude of faith. Then in Part Two we'll look at each of them in more detail.

In Part Three we'll consider steps we can take to keep a perspective of faith strong, once we understand what it is. In Part Four we'll look at the fascinating area of God's miraculous intervention in our lives and suggest what it means to have a reasonable expectation of the miraculous. Few areas help more to bolster our faith.

Then in the remaining three sections we'll consider how a faith perspective applies to some major areas of life: rebounding from disappointment, gaining focus for steps of faith and confronting the fears of change which hold us back from God's best.

Though many other topics could be considered in a study of this sort, I've chosen some which relate to areas where Christians struggle most frequently today. As I think is obvious from the menu

Nelson's instinctive reaction was not anger but awe. "I was as-tounded to think that I had driven all the way from Illinois with a faulty axle and nothing happened," he said. "If it had snapped at high speed on an interstate, I could have been killed." He then added, almost as an afterthought, that he found it impossible to feel much anxiety over how he would afford another major repair. "The same God who protected my life in this incident will provide the money needed to fix my car," he explained.

Both Jennifer and Nelson experienced significant personal set-backs which led them to reflect about God's purpose in what had happened. But while Jennifer concluded that God had turned against her, Nelson assumed God had done him a favor. Their conclusions could hardly have been farther apart.

I should hasten to say that I do not condemn Jennifer for her reaction. She is making the effort to think things through from the standpoint of her relationship with Christ, and I admire her hon-esty. She is a new Christian, and with her openness to expressing honestly what she is thinking and feeling, she may well work things through to a more positive perspective.

Yet while I respect Jennifer's way of thinking, I *envy* Nelson's. His is the sort of intensely hopeful outlook which I long to have characterize my own life and wish to hold out as a role model to others.

One reason I envy Nelson's manner of thinking is that I know the benefits this sort of mindset brings. When we're viewing God's work in our lives optimistically, we feel encouraged; our anxieties are lifted, we regain a sense of hope, we start seeing hidden serendipities in otherwise frustrating circumstances. Often, too, we see solutions to problems that seem insurmountable when we're thinking less optimistically.

The effects of this optimism spill over into many areas of our lives. Nelson's experience with the car has even had a positive ef-fect on the way he looks at relationships. Though he recently went through a difficult breakup, he is viewing the situation positively now, convinced that God kept him from a lifetime commitment with someone who was not compatible with him. "I'm confident that a God who loves me this much will provide for my relationship needs too," he added. This confidence has spurred him to become more active socially, and he is seeing opportunities for relationships which he hadn't recognized before.

A Basis for Optimism

But while I envy Nelson's perspective because of its benefits, I admire it most of all because it seems to represent so well the attitude of heart which the Scriptures term *faith.* Throughout the Bible we are urged to view God and his involvement in our lives through the eyes of faith. Though the concept of faith is never defined precisely in Scripture, it always seems to imply optimism—even blazing optimism—about what God is doing in our experience. The basis for this optimism includes not only the facts of Christ's salvation, forgiveness and empowering, but also the fact of God's protection and provision in our lives *individually.* The Scriptures stress that he is working out a distinctive plan for each of us, with our best interests and his highest intentions in mind. To say the least, this is a basis for considerable optimism!

This isn't to say that optimism in Scripture knows no bounds. The Bible has plenty to say about the other side of the coin and never comes close to a "don't-worry-be-happy" philosophy. Grief has an important place and is even recommended when one is coming to terms with a major loss (Acts 8:2). We're warned against falling into unrealistic fantasies which keep us from taking proper responsibility for our lives (Judg 18:27; 2 Thess 3:6-13). And we're urged to respect the power of sin and to fear the inevitable consequences if we cave in to its enticements. The man who is considering an affair with someone else's wife will be served well by a healthy dose of pessimism (Prov 7:6-27). So will the woman who is convinced she can achieve salvation by her own efforts (Rom 3:23).

Still, when it comes to considering the work of God in our lives as Christians, the accent in Scripture is strongly on optimism. This optimism is at the heart of what the Bible means by faith.

Less Help Than We Need

One of my frustrations with the modern church is that so little teaching is directed at explaining what faith is. Paul declares that "faith comes from hearing" (Rom 10:17). Yet many churches teach extensively about doctrinal issues—matters of *the* faith —but little about what it means to have an *attitude* of faith. Some pastors and teachers fear that the area is simply too subjective for formal preaching and teaching. Other churches emphasize our responsibility as Christians to serve God yet give little attention to the spirit of faith which inspires good works.

Churches which do present regular teaching on faith often feature messages high on anecdotes and low on biblical content, which fail to address the questions that more thoughtful Christians raise. At the most unfortunate extreme are churches which emphasize positive thinking or—even worse—a "name-it-and-claim-it" philosophy. "Create your own reality by believing it can happen!" is what is proclaimed. These "what-you-believe-you-can-achieve" notions distort the biblical understanding of faith into a human tool for getting what you want through yanking God's chain. Thinking Christians usually see through the façade but are often left confused about what the relationship between faith and optimism actually is.

The absence of clear and constructive teaching on faith in many churches is unfortunate, for next to the triumph of grace, the importance of faith is the most significant and pervasive theme in the Bible. Scripture minces no words in stressing that faith is central to our ability to relate to God on every level. While we are saved by grace, it is grace *through faith* (Eph 2:8; Rom 3:22-25; Rom 5:1; Gal 3:26; 2 Tim 3:15). We are called not merely to obey God but to the obedience *of faith* (Rom 1:5; 16:26; Heb 11). It is through faith that we become righteous before God (Rom 3:22; Phil 3:9), enjoy a personal relationship with Christ (Eph 3:17), are enabled to pray effectively (Eph 3:12) and become able to understand otherwise puzzling matters of doctrine (Heb 11:3). We experience God's protection through faith (1 Pet 1:5) and put ourselves in position to enjoy all of the other benefits that he extends to us (Gal 3:22; Heb 6:12). Indeed, the writer of Hebrews states it most inclusively in saying, "Without faith it is impossible to please God" (Heb 11:6).

Given the extraordinary extent to which Scripture extols faith and our need for it, it is important for us as Christians to give close and frequent attention to what an attitude of faith is and to whether our life is reflecting it. Far too often our instinctive reaction to challenges is like Jennifer's rather than Nelson's. We each have an ongoing, chronic and desperate need for the rekindling of our faith and for experiencing the optimism which faith inspires.

Where We're Heading
My hope in writing this book is to make a contribution to that process. One thing I want to do is consider specifically what a perspective of faith involves. In the next chapter we will consider four outlooks which are central to the biblical attitude of faith. Then in Part Two we'll look at each of them in more detail.

In Part Three we'll consider steps we can take to keep a perspective of faith strong, once we understand what it is. In Part Four we'll look at the fascinating area of God's miraculous intervention in our lives and suggest what it means to have a reasonable expectation of the miraculous. Few areas help more to bolster our faith.

Then in the remaining three sections we'll consider how a faith perspective applies to some major areas of life: rebounding from disappointment, gaining focus for steps of faith and confronting the fears of change which hold us back from God's best.

Though many other topics could be considered in a study of this sort, I've chosen some which relate to areas where Christians struggle most frequently today. As I think is obvious from the menu of topics, my concern is not with examining Christian doctrine per se, but with considering how we should view our life experience from the standpoint of faith. That area alone will give us more than enough concerns for one book.

My purpose in this book is not only to consider what faith is, but to *encourage* faith. Each chapter is written both to add something to our understanding of faith *and* as a meditation to inspire faith. To that end I have kept the chapters brief, following a format used in my monthly newsletter for the past fifteen years. All of these chapters have appeared in the newsletter and represent my best effort to encourage faith in friends and fellow Christians— many whom I know well—and in myself

I believe you will derive the greatest benefit from these chapters if you read them reflectively. Take some time after each one to consider its biblical insights and whether they touch a point of need in your own life. Is there a way in which your outlook on God and his role in your life needs to be adjusted? Ask God for the grace to see that area from the standpoint of faith and to have a more abiding perspective of faith at that point.

My earnest hope is that God will use these reflections to help you see your life more consistently with the eyes of faith. May the Lord bless you richly as you read.

Transferable Faith

One further thought before we move ahead. Nelson reached his impressive convictions of faith by following a simple line of reasoning: *If God has proven trustworthy in one circumstance, he can be trusted in another.* I am certain that this ability to transfer the lessons learned from one experience to another is at the heart of all successful living.

It's the basis for the counsel offered by Richard Bolles in his classic job-seeking manual *What Color Is Your Parachute?*[1] Bolles urges us to see our skills as "transferable." If you've been successful as a waiter, for instance, you've learned abilities which can be employed in more challenging situations. You've developed inter-personal and communication skills which could be used in management or teaching positions.

Just as we need to see our talents as transferable, we also should regard our experiences of faith as being so. We should strive to remember the lessons learned about God's faithfulness in one situation and apply them in new circumstances. While this may seem to be an elementary point, it's not at all natural for us to think in this way. Consider that on numerous occasions Jesus had to reteach his disciples lessons they had already supposedly learned and should have been applying in new situations.

On the positive side, David is an inspiring example of how the lessons of faith can be transferred from one situation to another in his decision to fight Goliath. He assumed that God would give him success because of the protection he had experienced in shepherding. "The LORD who delivered me from the paw of the lion and the paw of the bear will deliver me from the hand of this Philistine," David concluded (1 Sam 17:37).

This is the manner of thinking we need to apply to all the challenges we face. This is the sort of thinking that's at the heart of authentic faith. For each of us it boils down to an exceedingly encouraging point: *The same God who has supported us in the past, who met the needs of those in Scripture, who faithfully takes care of so many people whom we know—this same God will protect us in all our challenges and provide for us as we take steps of faith.* There is scarcely a more significant thought we can grasp than this. Let us take great encouragement from it and be inspired to live courageously.

2

Outrageous Faith

I *once learned an unforgettable lesson from an invoice that* I received in the mail. It was from the insurance company which provides health and pension coverage for our ministry. Several months earlier I had petitioned them, asking that they cut our quarterly payment of $1,500 in half. In reading their literature I had discovered a provision which indicated this was possible under certain conditions, which I felt we met. Reducing the payment this much would be a considerable help financially to our ministry, which was still in its early stage.

The company's brochure was ambiguous, though, and I wasn't at all certain they would grant my request. I carefully crafted a letter explaining why I thought we qualified, then followed it up with about a half-dozen phone calls. I also asked that the change be retroactive and they reimburse us for past overpayments. In the end I felt I was getting nowhere, fighting an enormous bureaucracy with no concern for the little guy.

Finally their invoice arrived. I confess that my faith was at less than mustard-seed intensity as I opened the envelope. Frankly, I expected the worst. Indeed, as I read their statement I found my negative expectations rewarded. It was a bill for $1,500—simply business as usual. All of my effort to change things had been to no avail.

It was not until several days later that I reread the statement and realized I had overlooked one small detail. Following the "$1,500" were two letters—"CR"—the abbreviation for "CREDIT." They were not billing us $1,500 but *refunding* us that amount!

The invoice, in short, revealed that I had *succeeded* in petitioning the company. But in my skeptical spirit I had read it to say just the opposite.

The Perils of Pessimism

It is an understatement to say that our expectations dramatically affect our view of reality. When we expect a positive outcome, we're alert to indications of success that come our way. But when we expect failure, we can miss the signs of success altogether or even read them mistakenly as proofs of defeat. As my experience with the invoice shows, missing some small detail can make all the difference in how we interpret a situation.

It's to this end that the Scriptures warn us so frequently of the extreme dangers of hardness of heart. "Hardness of heart" is the biblical term for loss of optimism, particularly regarding our expectations of God. When hardness of heart sets in, a crust forms over our mind and feelings; gradually we stop thinking creatively and begin seeing everything from a negative perspective. We cease believing that God has our best interests in mind and start drawing restrictions around his possibilities for our life and the lives of others.

While Scripture urges us to be alert to the problem of hardness of heart, it stresses even more emphatically that we can avoid its hazards through an outlook of faith. Faith is the diametrical opposite of hardness of heart. While the one expects the worst of God, the other expects the best of him. Faith is an exceedingly hopeful, trusting and confident perspective. From the viewpoint of faith we see our lives not only realistically but optimistically as well. The small details which signify God's care and provision for us are much less likely to escape our notice.

Had my expectations been more faith-inspired when I first examined that invoice, I doubt I would have been so quick to misinterpret it. The experience stands out in my mind as a classic example of what happens when our faith is insufficient—a lesson I've never forgotten.

The Rewards of Faith

Since our need for faith is so deep-seated, we should make every effort to understand as clearly as possible what an attitude of faith involves. What are the characteristics which make up an outlook of faith? Understanding them will allow us to gauge whether we are seeing our own life from the standpoint of faith or not.

Some of the most valuable insights which Scripture provides into the nature of faith come through examples of those who demonstrated it. While there are many such examples in the Old and New Testaments, I find it particularly helpful to look at those where Jesus directly complimented someone's faith. Surprisingly, such situations are not common in the Gospels. Though Jesus spoke often *about* faith, he *commended* the faith of individuals on only eight occasions. The fact that he was so sparing in affirming people's faith suggests that those instances when he did are supreme demonstrations of faith. Taken together, they should give us a treasured insight into the characteristics of faith. These incidents include the following people:

Blind Bartimaeus. As Jesus is leaving Jericho, a blind beggar sitting by the roadside repeatedly cries to him for mercy, even though numerous people admonish him to be quiet. Jesus invites the man to come to him and asks him his request. When he replies, "Rabbi, I want to see," Jesus responds, "Go, your faith has healed you" (Mk

10:46-52; Lk 18:35-43).

A woman with a hemorrhage. A woman who has experienced a blood flow for twelve years decides to approach Jesus for help. She pushes through a massive crowd and when she reaches Jesus merely touches the edge of his robe. Her hemorrhaging instantly stops. Recognizing that someone has drawn on his healing power, Jesus looks around the crowd, asking who has touched him. When the woman, now terrified, admits her deed, he declares, "Daughter, your faith has healed you. Go in peace and be freed from your suffering" (Mk 5:25-34; Mt 9:20-22; Lk 8:43-48).

Four men with a paralyzed friend. Four men, eager to bring their disabled friend to Jesus for healing, are unable to forge through a dense, unyielding crowd to reach Jesus in the home where he is teaching. In a burst of ingenuity, they pull tiles off the roof above the room where Jesus is sitting and lower the man in front of him. The Gospel writers note that "when Jesus saw their faith," he immediately turned his attention to this man, forgiving his sins and healing him (Mk 2:1-12; Mt 9:1-8; Lk 5:17-26).

A tenacious woman. A Canaanite woman persists in begging Jesus to heal her demon-possessed daughter, in spite of the fact that he initially seems reluctant to get involved. Finally he agrees to help her, exclaiming, "Woman, you have great faith! Your request is granted" (Mt 15:21-28).

A disdained woman. A prostitute enters a Pharisee's home where Jesus is dining and stands behind Jesus weeping. Finally she kneels and, drenching his feet with her tears, kisses them, perfumes them and wipes them with her hair. Jesus admonishes his host for despising this woman, then turns to her and says, "Your sins are forgiven. . . . Your faith has saved you; go in peace" (Lk 7:36-50).

The one leper who thanks Jesus. Ten lepers approach Jesus and ask for healing. He tells them to go and present themselves to the priest. As they are walking away their leprosy disappears. One man—the only Samaritan among this group of Jews—rushes back to Jesus and falls at his feet, thanking him and praising God profusely. Jesus, astonished that none of the others has displayed such gratitude, says to the man, "Rise and go; your faith has made you well" (Lk 17:11-19).

A centurion who requests healing for his servant. A Roman military official sends a group of Jewish officials to ask Jesus to come to his home and heal his critically ill servant. Jesus agrees to go but while traveling there is met by a delegation of the centurion's friends who revise the request. The centurion doesn't want to burden Jesus with the journey, they say, and feels unworthy for him to enter his home. He asks that Jesus simply perform the miracle from this distance. Just as soldiers obey his own orders without hesitation, the centurion reasons, his servant's spirit will respond to Jesus' command for healing even without Jesus being physically present. The centurion's thoughtfulness and creative reasoning amaze Jesus and evoke the most effusive comment he makes in the Gospels about anyone's faith: "I tell you, I have not found such great faith even in Israel" (Lk 7:2-10).

Two blind men who ask for healing. Two blind men follow Jesus as he travels along and implore him to heal them. Finally he queries them, "Do you believe that I am able to do this?" When they reply, "Yes," he responds, "According to your faith will it be done to you." At that moment their sight is restored (Mt 9:27-29).

Four Characteristics of Faith

These are the sum total of incidents in the Gospels where Jesus explicitly compliments someone's faith. Perhaps most surprising is that in none of them did the person's faith have anything to do with doctrinal knowledge. Most of these people had only an elementary grasp of who Jesus was, and none had anything close to a highly developed Christian theology. The faith which impressed Jesus in every case, rather, was an attitude of heart. Most obviously it amounted to an uncanny optimism about the possibility of receiving help from him.

When we look more closely at the attitude of faith these people displayed, we find it involved at least four specific outlooks:

√ *1. The belief that Jesus was a friend who desired the very best for them.* It is more instinctive to think of God as our adversary than our friend, especially during times of personal disappointment or loss. Faith is an attitude which holds fast to the conviction that God is an unequivocal friend who wills good, not evil, for us.

2. The belief that they would benefit by seeking help from Christ and submitting to him. We often hear it said that Christians should serve Christ without any hope for reward. The Scriptures, however, know nothing of such rigid legalism. Rather, they speak extensively of the benefits which derive from a relationship with Christ and urge us to earnestly seek and desire these advantages (Heb 11:6). Faith desires the greatest benefits God offers and believes these will result from faithfully following Christ. It is "the will to live" in the highest sense. Perhaps better stated, it is the will to live *abundantly.*

3. The determination to do whatever was necessary to get help from Jesus. The faith these people demonstrated was strongly active, not merely passive—as many Christians assume faith should normally be. This is impressive considering that individuals in at least six of these cases had to overcome significant obstacles, social pressure or stigma to approach Jesus. Their examples show that faith often involves taking significant personal initiative.

4. Considerable confidence that their specific need would be met by Jesus. They were highly optimistic about accomplishing their purpose. Their confidence did stop short of a "what-you-believe-you-can-achieve" philosophy; I don't sense that most of them were blatantly certain they would reach their goal. Yet they were all strongly confident that Jesus was *able* to solve their particular problem (Mt 9:28) and exceedingly hopeful he would do so. Their attitude is perhaps best described as *substantial optimism* that they would get their needs met. This substantial optimism is at the heart of authentic faith.

I believe that these four outlooks go a long way toward describing the attitude of faith as Scripture understands it. They are good benchmarks for measuring how well our own attitudes compare with genuine faith. This is not to imply that developing our knowledge of doctrine is unimportant or unrelated to experiencing faith. Christians who are growing in faith will be motivated to grow in their doctrinal understanding as well—to strengthen their grasp of "the faith." Still, the *attitude* of faith is something much more basic and may be experienced by even a new Christian or one with minimal doctrinal insight. It is best described as *an optimistic expectation about receiving help from God.* The four outlooks we've examined throw further light on what this attitude of faith involves.

The Challenge of Faith

We will take a closer look at each of these perspectives in the next section. You and I will do well to adopt these viewpoints and hold fast to them, as we face challenges in the present and as we plan for our future. Great benefit comes from spending some uncluttered time each day in personal reflection, carefully considering in what ways our own faith is inadequate and reminding ourselves of the basis we have for staying hopeful. Let me encourage you to invest such time.

And during the course of the day, when you find yourself slipping into a pessimistic frame of mind, make a practice of stopping yourself and noting where you are falling short of an optimistic outlook. Remind yourself of the benefits that come from an attitude of faith: you see both your present situation and your future possibilities more clearly. And ask God to renew this attitude within you.

I urge you to make every effort to see your life through the eyes of faith.

It's to your credit.

II

Optimism
and Faith

3

Friend or Foe?
Our Shifting
View of God

L*ast summer our family spent a week vacationing at* Chincoteague Island. One afternoon when Nate and I were driving down Main Street, he noticed the Ben Franklin store in the center of the old business district. The original sign still spans the storefront, with the name "Ben Franklin" in the center and the slogan "5-10" in a circle on either side. Nate glanced at the sign and then, puzzled, asked, "Why is that store only open from 5:00 to 10:00?"

At first I thought my eleven-year-old boy was joking. But he was serious, and I quickly realized why. To a boy raised in the era of "7-11" and "6-12" marts—stores which included their original hours of operation on large signs as part of their names—it was only natural to assume that two hyphenated numbers on a store sign indicated when it was open. Since five-and-ten-cent stores were commonplace in my childhood, on the other hand, it never dawned on me that the sign could be read in any way other than intended.

(Nate told me he had never heard of a five-and-ten-cent store. When I tried to explain the concept to him, he found it bizarre. For a child living in a time when candy bars are fifty cents and comic books a dollar, this response isn't hard to understand.)

The Problem of Filters

The incident is but one small example of a truth that we experience in much more profound ways every day of our lives. It's the fact that we interpret what we see and experience through filters. By "filters" I mean certain ingrained perspectives through which we sift our impressions and that dramatically affect our conclusions. Nate's deduction about the Ben Franklin sign—however misplaced—makes perfect sense once his filter is understood.

This doesn't mean, of course, that our filters always work against us. When our assumptions are accurate, so are our conclusions. Clear filters lead to clear perceptions. Yet too often our filters are clouded by misleading notions, which lead us to conclusions that hit wide of the mark of reality.

This fact has critical implications for our walk of faith. Apart from the benefit of biblical revelation, we see God through an unfortunate filter: we instinctively think of him as our adversary, not our friend. We assume that he dislikes us; he is displeased with us; only through the most heroic effort to live an exemplary life can we possibly hope to win his favor. Even then we fear that he is probably too busy with global concerns to take an interest in the details of our life.

The gospel message strongly challenges our natural assumptions about God. It declares that he loves us infinitely and takes such providential control of our lives that whatever happens is to our benefit (Rom 8:28). It provides us with an exceedingly positive filter for viewing God and his work in our lives.

Yet the "adversary filter" is already powerfully in place. Add to this the extreme limitations of our understanding: when it comes to knowing what God is doing behind the scenes in our lives, we see only the tip of the iceberg. The result is that we're prone to think his hand has turned against us whenever we experience a setback or disappointment

Most of us find that our view of God vacillates considerably. When things seem to be going well, we assume that he is pleased with us and affirming us—that he is our good friend and companion. When circumstances appear unfavorable, we assume that our worst fears are being confirmed: God doesn't like us after all. He's finally getting even with us and working to thwart our plans.

Even when obvious blessings occur, it's natural to fear that they are aberrations from how God normally deals with us. I'll never forget how a friend of mine once put it. Rob was scheduled to fly his wife and son from Washington, D.C., to Cumberland, Maryland, in his small plane. But at the last minute a squabble over who would ride in the tiny back seat provoked Rob to drive his family to Cumberland rather than fly.

As he was returning to Washington, a fierce storm struck the region. Many of the small aircraft at the suburban airport where Rob keeps his plane were overturned and damaged. Ironically, the squall arose at just the time when Rob would have arrived back there if he had been flying. Since the storm had not been predicted, he probably would have flown into the middle of it.

When Rob shared this incident with me, he spoke exuberantly about how God had protected him. "I'm finally beginning to think that God must like me," he said. He added, though, that he had a nagging fear that maybe—just maybe—God had provided this blessing to catch him off guard. Perhaps he was just setting him up for a future disaster—fattening him up for the kill, so to speak. "Frankly, I fear the Big One is coming," he confessed.

Wrong Conclusions

The fear which Rob expressed captures so well an attitude toward God which is often displayed by individuals in Scripture. We see examples of individuals misinterpreting God's intentions throughout the Bible. This is true with many who were involved in the events of Jesus' birth, for instance. Most who heard news related to it reacted with fear or disappointment to the information they received. Although God intended to bless them exceedingly, they initially read things quite differently and feared the worst.

When the angel appeared to Zechariah to announce that his wife would bear a son, Zechariah "was startled and was gripped with fear" (Lk 1:12). And it made little difference that the angel who visited Mary strongly affirmed her, saying, "Greetings, you who are highly favored! The Lord is with you." Mary's response was still one of dread. She "was greatly troubled at his words and wondered what kind of greeting this might be" (Lk 1:28-29). Likewise, when the angel confronted the shepherds, they were filled with terror rather than elation—even though "the glory of the Lord shone around them" (Lk 2:8-14).

Joseph's reaction to the first news of Mary's pregnancy, too, is interesting to consider. When he heard that she was expecting, he assumed she'd been promiscuous and decided to break off their engagement (Mt 1:18-19). His reaction is understandable, since it was based only on the information which he had. Yet the incident reminds us of how our initial assumptions are often based on very inadequate information. What at first appears to be a setback may be the doorway to a great blessing.

Of course, the most tragic example of someone concluding that God was against him was Herod. He feared that Jesus would usurp his authority. Herod wasn't the only one disturbed about the political implications of Christ's birth, to be sure, but "all Jerusalem with him" was troubled (Mt 2:3). It seems that most people of the time viewed the news of Jesus' arrival as anything but auspicious. Yet Herod is the one who, in his sweeping murder of the male babies in Bethlehem, best epitomizes the dreadful consequences which can result from perceiving God's work through the adversary filter.

The biblical account of Christ's birth reveals the human reactions of the participants—but even more importantly, it shows the gracious response of God to these people. God did not abandon Zechariah, Mary, Joseph or the shepherds to their dubious reactions but continued to instruct them, giving them the insight they needed to understand his true intentions. What an encouraging reminder this is that God doesn't leave us to our negative moods and skeptical assumptions but continues to give us wisdom to see things from his viewpoint—the renewal of our minds which Paul speaks of in Romans 12:2.

Indeed, the fact that God became human in Christ is the supreme reminder of how fully committed he is to relating to us in our human condition, to meeting our needs and to working out a plan for each of us that reflects his best for our life. These thoughts are implied by the prophetic name given Jesus at his birth—*Immanuel,* meaning "God with us" (Mt 1:23).

Beyond First Impressions

All of this presents us with a considerable challenge as Christians. Since our tendency to view God in adversary terms is so deep-rooted, we need to make a continual effort to concentrate on the grace-centered perspective of Scripture. We need to remind ourselves constantly that God does have our best interests in mind in every situation we encounter. We may be totally unable to see how this can be true, but that doesn't change the reality of it.

And we need to remember the lessons we've learned from experience of God's grace and protection. It's especially helpful to recall those times when our negative impressions of what God was doing proved mistaken, or when an apparent calamity proved to carry hidden blessings.

Last summer my friends Russ and Marguerite Hermanson had a dreadful experience. During a fierce thunderstorm, lightning struck the chimney of their home. The lightning bolt not only demolished the standing portion of the chimney but sent a blast of current throughout the house, destroying about thirty appliances and scorching walls and furniture. A hair dryer that wasn't even plugged in blew out, since its plug was touching a baseboard heater that became a conductor of the lightning's current.

Tall trees surround the Hermansons' home. Since lightning usually hits the highest target, the fact that it struck their chimney rather than one of the oaks was puzzling. Russ and Marguerite could naturally have interpreted the event as a sign of God's judgment, especially since lightning is a classic metaphor for God's wrath.

Yet the Hermansons have learned from long experience to recognize the subtle indications of God's protection in their lives. Almost immediately they saw serendipities in the calamity: though four children were asleep in their home that morning, none was injured, even though one lay perilously close to a scorched wall. In addition, no house fire resulted—odd, considering the severity of the strike.

Yes, the long period of cleaning and reconstruction that followed greatly inconvenienced Russ and Marguerite. Yet the process brought a far-reaching benefit which they could never have anticipated. While rebuilding the chimney, workers discovered that creosote had long been escaping through cracks to the outside portion of the flue liner, a problem resulting from faulty construction. Since the Hermansons heat their home with wood, the buildup of creosote between the chimney and the inside wall was considerable. Yet it had never been detected during the biannual chimney sweep.

Because creosote ignites under intense heat, the Hermansons were sitting ducks for a major house fire. Russ and Marguerite now view the lightning strike as a gracious act of God protecting their home and family, for apart from it the chimney defect wouldn't have been discovered. A small disaster saved them from a much greater one. It's enough to cause us all to revise the lightning metaphor a bit!

Reality Check

May God grant us the grace to see our lives from the standpoint of grace. May the biblical message of Christ's protection, provision, forgiveness and perfect love for us be the filter through which we interpret everything that happens to us. And may we have the divine capacity to think twice whenever we suspect that God is acting against us or loves us with less than the infinite love which Scripture promises. May we have the ability to change filters quickly whenever our view of God gets clouded by legalistic or punitive notions.

Let us strive for a view of God that never vacillates but sees him consistently as our closest friend. Far from an aberration, Christ's goodness to us is an ongoing reality each split second of our lives.

4

Serving Christ
For the (Highest)
Benefits

For more than twelve years Harold pastored a thriving evan-
gelical church. During his tenure a tiny congregation of less than a
hundred grew to nearly a thousand active members, a dynamic Christian community supporting programs for Christians of all ages.

Members of the church revered Harold for his moral integrity
and solid biblical teaching. He was not one to gloss over the hard
teachings of Scripture. He constantly emphasized responsibility to
God and the importance of rock-solid obedience to Christ. He was
quick to express his contempt for those who gave way to moral
failure and more than a few times insisted that backsliding members leave the church. He preached a "saved-to-serve" theology,
stressing that members should labor to the point of exhaustion in
evangelizing, recruiting and building up the church.

Church members and leaders alike were understandably stunned when one Sunday morning Harold, without previous notice, announced that he was resigning his position and the ministry effective in four weeks. The reason, he explained, was that he was burned out and needed to slow down for a while.

The next month felt like an extended wake for members of this devoted fellowship, who couldn't believe their trusted shepherd was leaving the flock.

Only after Harold preached his final sermon and endured his last farewell-tribute party did the truth finally come out. At a special meeting of the church board, convened at his request, Harold announced that he was leaving his marriage of twenty years and moving in with Sylvia, the church's choir director. This, he confessed, was why he had resigned.

Grief-stricken members of the board begged Harold to explain how he could abandon his wife and three teenage daughters, when this violated every principle he had preached about for years. Harold replied that he knew it was difficult for them to understand his decision. Yet Sylvia offered him happiness which he had never experienced in a relationship. She was sensitive to him in ways that his wife had never been, and there was romantic chemistry between them which had been long missing in his marriage. Harold admitted that what he was doing was wrong. He hoped, though, that God would be lenient with him, forgive him and provide for those he was leaving behind. "It's simply something I feel compelled to do, and that's the end of it," he finally said.

After Harold's brother, himself a member of the board, stood and tearfully pleaded with him to reconsider, Harold rose and calmly replied, "The decision is final." He then turned and walked out of the room.

When Strong Christians Fall

If you have walked with Christ for very long, you have undoubtedly witnessed a situation like this. A Christian whom you greatly respected suddenly and inexplicably turned against the principles he or she espoused. I have witnessed this tragedy so many times that I'm no longer shocked by it, though I'm always saddened when it happens. The "Harolds" I've known—or known about—have included pastors of large, dynamic churches, counselors, writers, choir directors, musical performers and leaders on many different levels in local church ministry. I'm not speaking of Christians who in a moment of weakness gave in to a temptation but later repented (which of us has not done this many times?). I'm referring to those who in a serious and far-reaching way turned their backs on what they knew to be God's will.

When Christians whom we esteem deliberately renege on their values, we are left shaking our heads in bewilderment. How could they possibly have caved in? They seemed so strong spiritually. They knew so much Scripture. They influenced so many others. They were so diligent in their Christian walk. What was missing?

While reasons vary from person to person, I'm convinced that in most cases the missing ingredient is *faith*. This may seem to be a simplistic answer. We tend to think that Christians who have a moral breakdown simply did not try hard enough. In reality, they often have made a valiant effort to follow Christian principles. Yet they were spurred on more by a sense of duty or loyalty than by a deep-seated conviction that they would truly *benefit* by obeying Christ. They thought of obedience as a legalistic requirement. They failed to believe that they would be happiest by staying faithful to Christ. Faith in the benefits of obedience was absent.

Serious Christians who have a major moral lapse often have been schooled in a sacrificial notion of following Christ. The message they have heard is, *Give all your strength to obeying Christ and never count the cost. Serve Christ dutifully without any hope for reward.* While such a perspective sounds noble in theory, it fails to inspire them when they face a significant challenge to their faith. Since they are motivated by the desire to be happy—as we all are— they give in. While they admit that they are violating principles which they have held dear, they are now moved by a stronger de-

sire than upholding their values—namely, to seek their own fulfillment.

Christians who are genuinely convinced that their welfare
depends upon faithfully following the Lord's will are much less
likely to give in to a significant temptation. Those who have been
taught to follow Christ without any expectation of reward, who have
constantly heard the do's and don'ts of Christianity proclaimed without an equal emphasis on the benefits of such obedience, may reach
the point where following Christ simply doesn't seem worth the
effort. They will conclude that being true to themselves and getting
a life means putting their Christian commitment on the back burner.

Our Motive for Following Christ

But what about the premise I'm suggesting? Is it right to say that
one should follow Christ for the sake of the benefits that result? Or
is this a vain and selfish motive? Is it better to live for him without
any expectation of reward? Which motive is the higher one?

For most Christians the push-button response is that our commitment to Christ shouldn't be based on any hope of personal advantage. *"You should serve God for nothing,"* as I heard it
proclaimed in a sermon. Yet this comes dangerously close to missing the essence of the biblical idea of faith.

Hebrews 11:6 declares, "Without faith it is impossible to please
God, because anyone who comes to him must believe that he exists
and that he rewards those who earnestly seek him." The writer states
that it's not merely *okay* to desire benefits from following Christ
but *necessary* if we're going to be able to live effectively for him.
Faith, as Scripture understands it, is an outlook which believes that
the rewards of following Christ are greater than those which come
from disregarding his will. Without the expectation of personal benefit, the motivation to stay faithful to Christ when his will strongly
conflicts with our own simply won't be there.

In his recently published *The Unity of the Bible,* Daniel P. Fuller
explores this concept of faith, which he notes permeates both the

Old and New Testaments. In a superbly helpful analogy, Fuller compares the relation between faith and obedience in Scripture to the attitude with which we follow a doctor's prescription. We obey a doctor's orders not because we're duty-bound to do so, but because we trust the doctor's insights and believe we will be better off by following his or her advice. This is precisely the motivation that should underlie our obedience to God.[1]

About ten years ago I had a terrifying experience. For one traumatic week my 20-20 eyesight gradually faded, growing dimmer each day, until it was 20-400—I was almost "legally blind." By the end of that week I could barely see to read or drive, and Evie was afraid to be in the car when I was behind the wheel. I was greatly relieved when an ophthalmologist not only diagnosed the problem (optic neuritis) but confidently prescribed a cure—the wonder drug prednizone. I eagerly took the first dose, then followed the prescribed regimen for several weeks, even though it meant discipline and the inconvenience of getting up in the night to take a pill. It was one of the greatest joys of my life to watch the world around me gradually come into focus again.

In this case my obedience to the doctor sprang from one motive—the belief that I would benefit from following his counsel. That belief, of course, involved faith—faith that his prognosis was correct.

I agree with Dan Fuller that this is how faith and obedience relate in Scripture. God gives us his diagnosis of our situation and prescribes a remedy. We follow it with the hope of improving our life. Our obedience flows from faith that God understands our condition better than we do and that his plan of action is infinitely better than any we could dream up on our own.

More Than Obligation

This motive differs from one which is often suggested as a basis for following Christ—that we have an *obligation* to do so. It's said that we should obey him simply from a sense of duty, without hope of reward.

I don't deny that obeying from obligation is better than not obeying at all. Yet somehow this brings to my mind inmates in a penal institution obeying out of desperation because they have no other choice. Surely this isn't the spirit in which Scripture calls us to "the obedience of faith" (Rom 1:5; 16:26), any more than I took the prednizone out of obligation to my doctor. I did so because I believed I would benefit as a result.

There's no question that we have an extraordinary obligation to Christ. But Scripture stresses that it cannot be fulfilled through compulsion but only through faith. "Without faith it is impossible to please God." When the primary motive for obedience is obligation to God, I lay myself bare to pride and a "works mentality," from thinking that I can fulfill my obligation to God through my own effort.

More Than Gratitude

A more subtle motive for obeying Christ which is sometimes suggested is gratitude. Because Christ has done everything for me, I ought to obey him out of gratefulness for his gift.

Of course we are called to undying gratitude to Christ. We ought to do everything possible to increase our thankfulness. But if gratitude is our *primary* motive for obedience, we're in trouble—just as I would have been if my only reason for taking the medicine was gratitude toward my physician. While I was extremely grateful for his help, gratitude would not have inspired me to swallow a single pill.

The young man who goes off to the mission field purely out of gratitude to Christ, for instance, runs at least two dangers. One is burnout, when the gratitude becomes hard to maintain. The other is—again—a works mentality, as he begins to think that he is somehow repaying Christ for what he has done.

My decision to go into missions—or into any profession — ought to be based on the conviction that I will be the most fulfilled and fruitful person possible in this role. If it be feared that this is a self-serving notion which will keep me from loving others effectively for Christ, I would argue just the opposite. We do our very best work for Christ when it's a reflection of our deepest levels of motivation. We give ourselves to others much more naturally, joyfully and creatively than when we're laboring purely from a sense of duty or gratitude.

Usually when those who are motivated and gifted for a vocation settle for another option which, say, seems less risky or more financially rewarding, the problem isn't that they are too concerned with their own happiness but *not concerned enough.* They settle for a measure of fulfillment that's less than what God holds forth for them. C. S. Lewis argues this point forcefully in his essay "The Weight of Glory":

> Indeed, if we consider the unblushing promises of reward and the staggering nature of the rewards promised in the Gospels, it would seem that our Lord finds our desires, not too strong, but too weak. We are halfhearted creatures . . . like an ignorant child, who wants to go on making mud pies in a slum because he cannot imagine what is meant by the offer of a holiday at sea. We are far too easily pleased.[2]

Don't Settle for Reduced Benefits

Our lack of confidence in the benefits of staying faithful to Christ is the problem behind most moral failure in the Christian life. The Christian man who believes as a matter of moral principle that he shouldn't cheat on his wife will obey that standard and tout it proudly as long as it's convenient to do so. Yet when an alluring opportunity comes along, to everyone's surprise he may give in. While he winces at renouncing the code he has held so highly, he is drawn by a higher motive—that of gaining happiness. Scripture teaches that he'll be happier staying faithful. Only if he believes in the depth of his heart that Scripture is right will he find the strength of will to turn his back on this immediate enticement.

Again, modern moralistic Christianity too often preaches the *requirements* of the Christian life without adequately stressing the *rewards* of obedience. It's little wonder that we see so much moral failure in the body of Christ today.

God has put within each of us the instinct for happiness. The desire to be happy is a God-given motive, inseparable from the will to live. Only as I come to believe that Christ's path for my life is infinitely better than any substitute will I have the sustained motivation to follow in his steps. The ultimate human problem is not disobedience but unbelief.

From this angle it becomes so important to continue doing those things that rekindle my enthusiasm for following Christ and for enjoying the benefits that come from obeying him. My devotional time, fellowship with other believers and regular worship experiences are so essential—not for "appeasing God" (another misplaced motive we could talk about) but because they help keep faith alive.

The greatest demonstration of this faith which looks to the reward is that of Jesus himself, "who for the joy set before him endured the cross, scorning its shame, and sat down at the right hand of the throne of God" (Heb 12:2). He couldn't see or feel that joy in those dark days when he steadfastly moved toward the cross. It was faith. Let us be inspired by his example.

5

Waiting in Faith vs. Stepping Out in Faith

Few questions confuse us more as Christians than what it means to live by faith. When does it mean sitting still and leaving a need completely in the hands of Christ? When does it mean taking prudent initiative to solve a problem or reach a goal?

Many serious Christians assume that faith usually means the former and not the latter. Jack longs for a new job which would make better use of his gifts. Yet he fears he would be pushing God by going out and looking for one. "Shouldn't I assume that if Christ wants me in a different job, he'll bring it along without any effort on my part?" he asks.

Susan, a woman who wants to be married, wrestles with a similar question. She would like to change jobs or even move to a different city where the prospects of meeting someone compatible are better. Yet she wonders if this would be taking matters too much into her own hands. Doesn't faith demand that she wait for Christ to bring the right man directly to her?

Both Jack and Susan would prefer to be doing something specific toward reaching their goals, and they each see clear steps they could take. They both feel frustrated and helpless in the face of dilemmas which they feel they could do something to remedy. Yet they fear that their efforts to change things would usurp God's authority. Surely faith must require that they sit still and wait for him to act.

I remember carrying this assumption as a young believer, yet I remember too the day when my thinking began to change. I'd been considering the possibility of beginning a radio ministry, which seemed a logical outgrowth of my experiences and contacts at the time. Yet I felt painfully guilty about doing anything direct to bring such a program about. I had heard so much talk about being still and waiting on the Lord that it seemed inconceivable he would want me to take any initiative toward this desire.

Finally I asked for the counsel of an older Christian whom I greatly respected. I really expected her to tell me to be passive and wait for the Lord to open any doors. To my surprise, she not only affirmed my dream but recommended I take some determined steps to follow it. Because I thought highly of her and knew she trusted strongly in Christ, I was left feeling much better about the matter of taking personal initiative. Though the radio ministry never got off the ground, her advice helped give me the strength of heart to pursue a music ministry and some other projects in my early years as a believer.

Over the years, though, I've continued to wrestle with the connection between being passive and being active as a Christian. When does faith require the one and when the other? It finally occurred to me several years ago that the relation between these two in Scripture is really much more straightforward and easy to understand than I had thought. Here is a way of explaining it that I am finding increasingly helpful.

The Two Levels of Faith

To begin with, we are called to exercise two different levels of faith at various times as believers. At one level we are to be inactive and wait patiently for the Lord to move. Here faith consists of believing that Christ will bring a solution apart from any effort on our end. It is shown in so many situations in Scripture where people were either told to be still or forced to be still and wait for the Lord to act. Examples include Joseph in prison, the Israelites at the edge of the impassable Jordan River, and Jesus' disciples when before his ascension they were instructed, "Do not leave Jerusalem, but wait for the gift my Father promised" (Acts 1:4).

Yet Scripture just as frequently affirms the faith involved in taking personal responsibility. There are so many impressive pictures in Scripture of individuals who, without any divine revelation or special prompting, took bold steps to reach a personal goal: Naomi and Ruth moving from Moab to Bethlehem, Nehemiah courageously organizing the Israelites to rebuild Jerusalem, Paul knocking on many doors to find opportunities to preach—in his own words, "making it my ambition to preach the gospel" (Rom 15:20 RSV).

In reality, there can be just as much faith involved in taking personal initiative as there is in waiting passively for the Lord to provide. While Ruth, for instance, would have been commended for staying in Moab and waiting for God to heal the heartbreak of her husband's death, she probably showed greater faith in going to Bethlehem. By moving forward she placed herself in a vulnerable position where she had to trust the Lord to protect her, to open doors and to make her venture successful. It is interesting that this very move opened her to the relationship with Boaz, who became her husband.

It is right, then, to speak of a second level of faith which we are to display as Christians. At this level we are active and assertive. We take initiative to find the answer to a need. And by moving forward we force ourselves to a dependence on the Lord which wouldn't be possible if we merely sat still.

While making this distinction is interesting enough, it still leaves the question, When does God want us to operate at level one faith and when at level two? Let me suggest a rule of thumb which I think applies in most cases: If we are facing a seemingly insurmountable problem—a situation which we perceive we are powerless to influence—we should stay at level one faith. Yet if there is a reasonable step we can take to improve things or to move toward a goal, then we should assume God wants us to operate at level two. This only makes sense considering that as we function at level two faith there is always plenty of opportunity for experiencing level one faith as well. As we move forward unexpected obstacles always arise which throw us back to waiting on the Lord.

If you examine most of the examples in Scripture where individuals did the will of God, you will find that they fit this pattern. Paul, for instance, generally assumed that he should take initiative to open doors except for those occasional times when God clearly closed them (Acts 16:6-7, 39-40).

Speaking Our Mind

We can expect, too, that taking personal initiative will frequently require us to express our convictions clearly—even to those who disagree with us—and that God will use our assertiveness to persuade people and open important doors for us. While we should always listen carefully to the counsel others give us and be open to having our insights changed by theirs, God will also use us to counsel them and at times to correct their misunderstandings. There is an interactive process here with which we need to become comfortable. We cannot simply assume that God will always want us to acquiesce if others are not immediately in favor of our plans. While we need to be considerate and compassionate when asserting ourselves at such times, we shouldn't be reluctant to express our convictions.

We find a wonderfully instructive example of such bold but courteous assertiveness in the biblical account of David interacting

with Saul about fighting Goliath. David took the initiative to pro-
pose that he battle the giant. Saul's initial response was negative:
"You are not able to go out against this Philistine and fight him;
you are only a boy, and he has been a fighting man from his youth"
(1 Sam 17:33). Most would have taken this admonition from the
most respected warrior in the land not only as wise counsel but as a
glorious reprieve from responsibility! David now had an easy out.
He had done his duty, declared his willingness to go into the heat of
battle, but was told he could stay on the sidelines. He could have
his cake and eat it too. He could glory in being the only person to
volunteer to fight the giant yet enjoy the freedom of not having to
face the challenge.

But David pressed his point with Saul:

Your servant has been keeping his father's sheep. When a lion
or a bear came and carried off a sheep from the flock, I went
after it, struck it and rescued the sheep from its mouth. When it
turned on me, I seized it by its hair, struck it and killed it. Your
servant has killed both the lion and the bear; this uncircumcised
Philistine will be like one of them, because he has defied the
armies of the living God. The LORD who delivered me from the
paw of the lion and the paw of the bear will deliver me from the
hand of this Philistine. (1 Sam 17:34-37)

Interestingly, Saul was not put off by David's straightforwardness.
To the contrary, he was changed by it. His response: "Go, and the
LORD be with you" (1 Sam 17:37). Even after that, David continued to be respectfully assertive with Saul. He urged that he be allowed to fight Goliath without the cumbersome armor Saul thought
he needed, and again Saul conceded. If David had taken the easy
out and passively accepted Saul's advice, not only would he have
stifled his own development but a nation of people would have
suffered for his silence. This is, in my opinion, the most helpful
example we find in Scripture of healthy assertiveness. We see God
honoring the efforts of one man to convince an individual considerably more knowledgeable and powerful than himself that he has

gifts which should be recognized and put to use. An entire nation benefited from his straightforwardness.

The passage drives home a point vital for each of us. Not only does God bring us to see broader opportunities for investing our lives, but he uses us as agents of change to bring these options about. Walking in faith requires that we assert ourselves. We can find the courage to do this if we believe that God will honor our efforts and that others will benefit from our initiative. David's example gives us rich encouragement at this point.

Pacing Yourself

Let me offer two cautions regarding taking personal initiative. One is that we should consider a step of faith only if we can pursue it without frenzy, within the time and energy limits the Lord has given us and without jeopardizing other commitments we have already made. The other is that our understanding of which steps of faith we should take should grow out of a regular—preferably daily— time alone with Christ, where we carefully think through the direction of our life and what God wants us to do. In general, individuals in Scripture were judged presumptuous not because they took personal initiative but because they did so without establishing their plans before the Lord (Josh 9:14).

Then, as we daily seek the Lord's direction, we should feel great freedom to take bold initiative to find the best opportunities for using our gifts and building relationships. I remember what great relief I felt as a young Christian when my friend suggested to me that it was okay to do this. I hope you will feel similar relief in realizing the freedom Scripture gives you at this point. The fact is that God gives us greater control to change the circumstances of our lives than we tend to think.

6

When Is a Door Really Closed?

A certain man made the national news this past week for an atypical reason: he passed his bar exam. While passing the bar is a notable achievement, it doesn't normally attract the attention of the national media. Yet his case was unique, for this tenacious soul had failed the test forty-seven previous times. Now, at age sixty, he finally passed on his forty-eighth try.

That's not all. The man noted in an interview that he hopes to embark on a twenty-year career as an attorney. As proof of his earnestness, he has purchased a briefcase!

I always find examples like his inspiring, for they bring to mind how some of us by nature are late bloomers—and that it's okay to be so. We run on different clocks. God has a different timetable for each of us. While one person realizes a significant accomplishment early in life, another does so much later. Some never do reach their goals, forced by circumstances into quite a different path—but on God's timetable that too can become significant.

This man's example is extreme, unquestionably. We might conclude that he demonstrates stubbornness more than healthy determination and could have spent his energy in better ways. Still, it's hard not to admire his perseverance, which continued way beyond the point when most of us would have quit. Often, our tendency is to go to the opposite extreme—to give up after a setback or two, even when a reasonable possibility of success still exists.

Faith generates optimism, and the person who walks in faith stays hopeful about reaching a goal as long as this expectation is justified. Resilience, too, is involved in genuine faith: we're able to rebound from loss and disappointment and regain our confidence about succeeding.

I enjoyed introducing my father-in-law, Glenn Kirkland, as a case in point when speaking to a singles group recently. Since the topic of the evening was finding a marriage partner, Glenn was a natural role model to present to them. At age seventy-two he has just become engaged to be married again. I suggested that Glenn did much to open himself to this blessing through his attitude and the way he has managed his life. He stayed close to the Lord during the long battle with Alzheimer's disease which his first wife, Grace, suffered, and never turned a hard heart toward God after her death a year ago. Then during this past year he did something essential for anyone wishing to be married—he became socially active again. Through joining the choir at Fourth Presbyterian Glenn met Barbara Nielson, now his fiancée and an exceptional match for him.

Yes, I did emphasize to these folks that they wouldn't necessarily have to wait until age seventy-two to find a suitable partner. Still, they clearly found his example inspiring and an important reminder that the hand of God isn't shortened at any point in our lives. We must not be too quick to shut a door in any area before God is ready to do so.

Yet for thoughtful Christians this raises a nagging question. Just when should you assume that a door is truly closed? At what point must you conclude that God wants you to let go of a longstanding desire and simply accept things as they are?

Easily Discouraged

To be honest, it takes little disappointment in any area for us to conclude that God is against our succeeding. I recall talking to a woman who deeply wanted to be married yet feared that the opportunity had passed her by. Many of her friends had already taken the step, and the one relationship which held the prospects of marriage for her had ended. She wondered if God was indicating through it all that she should abandon her hope of marrying and set her heart on staying single. She was twenty-two.

Christians who move into their later twenties, thirties or beyond, wanting to be married but finding no suitable opportunity, are especially inclined to draw the conclusion which this young woman reached. They're even more likely to do so if they've experienced a number of broken relationships or rejections along the way. If you're in this position, it may seem in all sincerity that the most Christ-honoring, reverent assumption you can make is that God is telling you to forsake your hope for marriage. Surely obedience to him must require that you put this desire on the altar and learn to joyfully accept your singleness.

But then you witness an example that defies the norm. A friend, well into her adult years and survivor of many disappointments, suddenly and surprisingly finds an excellent opportunity for marriage. Once she is married and the dust clears, she declares that she is glad she never let go of her hope. She even claims that she sees value now in those past relationships which didn't work out, for through them she grew and developed the qualities which have allowed her finally to be happily married. God does indeed have different clocks for us, she insists; she's grateful for that and thankful that she waited.

And so you're thrown back to square one. Just how do you know when a door is still open and when it's clearly shut? Just when is God telling you to keep persevering and when to give up?

Perseverance Pays Off

One point is indisputable. Scripture is resplendent with examples of those who found doors open at points when many would have concluded they were bolted shut. As we read through the Bible, we find numerous instances where individuals reached important horizons late in life, or after repeated tries, or in spite of extreme obstacles. Sarah conceives a child when both she and Abraham are elderly, and a number of years later Abraham remarries after Sarah dies. Isaac's servants dig a well successfully after two major thwarted attempts. Joseph realizes his dream of leadership after years of servitude and imprisonment. Moses becomes a champion of his people forty years after his first passionate attempt utterly fails. David becomes king of Israel in spite of severe ridicule from his brothers, apathy from his father and numerous battles with Saul's forces. Hannah gives birth to many children long after her husband has accepted her barrenness and encouraged her to do the same. Ruth finds joy in a new marriage after her first husband dies; and Naomi, bereft of her husband and both sons, finds unexpected solace in a grandchild born to Ruth. Zechariah and Elizabeth are blessed with a child in their old age, and the angel declares that this gift is in response to their longstanding prayer.

It's examples like these, I suspect, which lead author Garry Friesen to claim that the Bible doesn't recognize the concept of closed doors. I came across this point recently when rereading his *Decision Making and the Will of God* and was intrigued with it. Friesen notes:

> Interestingly, though Christians today speak of doors that are "closed," Scripture does not. The need for open doors certainly implies the existence of some that are closed. But that doesn't seem to be the mentality of Paul. If he were sovereignly prevented from pursuing a plan, and yet the plan itself was sound, he simply waited and tried again later. He did not view a blocked endeavor as a "closed door" sign from God that his plan was faulty.[1]

Friesen's claim is provocative, for on one level Scripture does speak of closed doors, though it does not use the term per se. Consider Paul's odyssey in Asia and Bithynia, for instance: "Paul and his companions traveled throughout the region of Phrygia and Galatia, having been kept by the Holy Spirit from preaching the word in the province of Asia. When they came to the border of Mysia, they tried to enter Bithynia, but the Spirit of Jesus would not allow them to" (Acts 16:6-7). It's hard to read this passage and not conclude that some doors were firmly shut against Paul and his party, regardless of the language used. They made two valiant attempts to enter regions for ministry which didn't open to them. And they accepted without question that these doors were closed. "So they passed by Mysia and went down to Troas" (Acts 16:8).

Yet on a broader level the passage validates the very point Friesen is making, for Paul and his friends never let go of their overriding determination to evangelize and to look for the best opportunities available for doing so. Soon Paul received a vision at night through which he and his team were led into a fruitful period of ministry in Macedonia (Acts 16:9-40). (Fruitful, that is, at the cost of an arrest, a beating and a night in jail. Yet the work of God was accomplished through it all.)

Drawing on Paul's experience in Acts 16 and similar experiences of people of faith throughout Scripture, we can suggest a resolution to the question of when a door is truly closed. Specific individual opportunities may close to us, and the time may come when we must accept that such doors are truly shut. But we should be very slow ever to conclude that the door is permanently closed against our broader, long-term aspirations which are based on a sound understanding of our God-given gifts and areas of interest.

To cite the marriage decision as an example: I may desire to marry a particular person, yet God says no. I will need to accept this as an unequivocal no and stop pounding on that door. God may say no to twenty such possibilities! This doesn't mean that my basic, underlying desire to be married is inappropriate or that God is forever closing the door against marriage. Indeed, it may be that my twenty-first endeavor will succeed. To be sure, if there are clear lessons to be gleaned from past disappointments, I should learn them. Yet I still have a sound basis for staying hopeful and active in moving toward the dream of marriage.

The same point applies to pursuing career opportunities. Certain positions may not open to me. Certain geographical regions may be closed. This doesn't imply that my overriding vocational aspirations are out of line. If they are based on a clear understanding of how God has gifted and motivated me, then I have good reason to hold on to them and to continue to look for situations in which they can be fulfilled.

Hope vs. Fixation

This isn't to underestimate the challenge involved in accepting that a specific door is closed. Indeed, we can become fixated on a particular option's working out to the point of our own downfall. One of the earliest stories of Scripture underscores this point. Adam and Eve became obsessed with eating fruit from the one tree that God said they could not touch. The fact that this tree was off limits didn't mean that God forbade them to enjoy apples or other delicacies of nature. It was merely that this *specific* tree was out of bounds for them.

In the same way we may become fixated on a particular relationship. We may continue to hang onto the hope of its working out long after we have clear evidence that this person is unavailable or unsuitable for us. In this case, our need is to accept God's no and move on.

We can become fixated on other unrealistic dreams as well. I'll never forget a young man I met named Clarence—a singer-guitarist who led singing in his church. He was convinced God had told him he was going to receive a recording contract from a certain Christian record company, one of the largest and best-known firms. Even after the company rejected Clarence's audition tape, he continued to believe that he knew God's mind on the matter better than they did. He was sure they would one day change their mind and decide to record him. It did not seem to me, however, that Clarence had the distinctive sort of talent needed to interest a major record company. The tragedy about his obsession with the recording contract was that it misdirected his energy. He was not focusing on steps he realistically *could* take to develop and employ his gifts.

These cautions aside, the point remains that we have a strong basis for faith and hope when it comes to our long-term dreams and aspirations. When these are based on a good self-understanding and are general enough to allow for flexibility as they are fleshed out, we can feel great freedom to pursue them earnestly until a door finally opens. And we're not obliged to think that individual setbacks mean that God has forever shut the door on a dream itself.

III

Winning the
Daily Battle

7

Faith in the Fast Lane

Richard Halverson was one of the busiest pastors I've ever met, but one of the most available. When I asked him to speak to a class at my college, he readily agreed. But on the day when he was scheduled to visit, I discovered that his availability had an interesting limit.

We had agreed to drive together to the class. But on my way to the church to meet him, my decrepit Corvair began to overheat. By the time I arrived, its condition was serious. Fortunately I was fifteen minutes early for our 9:30 appointment. I spied Dr. Halverson sitting in his car reading, so I pulled alongside. By now the whining from my engine rivaled an air-raid siren.

To my astonishment, he did not even look up. He must be asleep, I thought. But then he turned a page in the book resting on his steering wheel—which I now could see was a Bible—then turned a page again. By now our vehicles were engulfed by a cloud of smoke which would have made Moses jealous. But he never showed the slightest distraction. Finally, at precisely 9:30, he prayed, shut the

Bible and climbed out of his car. The smoke had now cleared and my engine had quieted.

After greeting me, he suggested (to my relief) that we go in his car. During the half-hour drive to the college, we talked about many things. But he never once suggested that he had noticed any unusual noises or sights during his quiet time. And I never mentioned that I'd seen anything unusual either.

Good Timing

One reason the event is so memorable is that it occurred on my first spiritual anniversary. On that date just one year before, I had committed my life to Christ, largely because of Dr. Halverson's radio preaching. I am one of numerous people who have been touched by his ministry. But that morning God gave me a priceless insight into why he has been so remarkably effective for Christ. Beyond any gifts for ministry is the fact that he has made it a priority in his strenuous schedule to spend personal time with the Lord, regardless of what needs to be cleared away for this to happen. His attention to the Lord had become so fine-tuned that even the racket from my car did not distract him.

It might seem that he was indifferent—so bent on following his religious routine that nothing else mattered. But he is one of the most people-centered Christian leaders I've known. As pastor of a huge church, president of World Vision, and chaplain of the United States Senate, he has given himself relentlessly to others. But the wellspring of his life has been a commitment to Christ which surpasses even his commitment to people.

His life mirrors a principle which I once heard Gordon MacDonald express in an unforgettable sermon. While reflecting on the life of John the Baptist, he noted that John had a lot going against him; his social mannerisms were bizarre, for instance. Yet he spent great periods of time quietly before the Lord. This reminds us, MacDonald said, that God doesn't need a member of Congress, a dignitary or a corporation president to do his work. He will use anyone who is merely willing to take the time to listen.

After nearly thirty years of walking with Christ, I confess that making time to be quiet before him still takes more effort than I like to admit. It isn't that praying, Scripture study and being quiet in Christ's presence are hard work per se. Once I'm doing these things I enjoy them, and almost daily the Lord proves their benefit to me. What makes it hard is that I have to take my hands off of other things I could be doing at the time. For a workaholic this is always a challenge.

Gaining Perspective

About ten years ago Evie and I felt the need for a new home. While our townhouse would have been adequate under most circumstances, my ministry was operating out of it, and office space was not sufficient. Yet the real estate market was at its worst point in decades and interest rates were outlandish. We couldn't afford to move, and the prospects of selling our present home were nil.

For several months I spent much time studying the market and reading real estate brochures but only became increasingly discouraged. Finally it dawned on me that I hadn't spent any serious time praying about the matter. I set aside two hours to pray and seek the Lord's direction, even though it seemed an intrusion into my "busy" schedule. I decided to take a leisurely drive in the country as I prayed, a practice that I've often found helpful.

As I meandered around the rural highways of upper Montgomery County, I came upon a street I had never noticed before, even though I thought I knew every nook and cranny of this county where I've spent most of my life. On that street was a house for sale—a house which immediately seemed right for our needs! But it would surely be too expensive. Within a week the owner accepted a contract from us; the price was considerably below market value. Within another week our townhouse sold, in spite of the fact that identical homes in our community had been on the market for months without selling.

The lesson is not that my prayers bent God's mind and con-
strained him to do something he wouldn't otherwise have wanted
to do. This was not the "health and wealth gospel" at work. What
happened during those several hours, I believe, was that God was
able to command my attention and show me a way to solve an "impossible" problem. He could just as well have given me grace to
accept things as they were. In fact, that has happened far more frequently than the more dramatic sort of answer which came on this
occasion.

But whatever his solution, I find again and again that it takes
time being still before him to be able to understand it.

Whether you are a student, a homemaker or someone involved
in a career, I urge you not to think of time devoted to being alone
with Christ as time taken away from the demands of your work.
View it, rather, as time invested with One who is able to give you
peace and wisdom to carry out your work effectively.

But remember that Satan will do everything possible to make
you regard it as an intrusion on your schedule. If that tactic doesn't
work, then he will bring into your time with Christ interruptions
which seem to demand immediate attention. Keep in mind that usually the problems can wait a few minutes while you put first things
first.

And when you do, you may just find that the smoke clears away
by itself.

8

Self-Talk:
How Much Can We
Psych Ourselves Up?

Few biblical incidents do more to ignite my faith than the story about the woman with the hemorrhage. For twelve years she experienced the indescribable discomfort and embarrassment of a blood flow which no physician could heal. To add to her misery, she became financially destitute, bankrupt from her extensive medical expenses. Mark summarizes the woman's despair in a sentence: "She had suffered a great deal under the care of many doctors and had spent all she had, yet instead of getting better she grew worse" (Mk 5:26).

Finally, after this interminable search for help, she heard of Jesus and his exceptional power to heal. She pressed through a dense crowd to touch him, and at the instant when her hand made contact with his clothing she was cured.

This woman's example inspires me because I identify so easily with her humanity. She apparently was terribly frightened as she approached Jesus, for unlike most others in the Gospels who sought healing from him she attempted to do so unnoticed—by merely brushing the edge of his robe. Yet Jesus recognized instantly that healing power had escaped from him. When he asked who had touched him, "the woman, knowing what had happened to her, came and fell at his feet and, trembling with fear, told him the whole truth" (Mk 5:33).

Given her intense fear, it's all the more impressive that she found the resolve to approach Jesus for healing. It's this display of courage which impresses me most. I'm moved, too, by her incredible optimism: in spite of her constant experience of disappointment during more than a decade of seeking help from medical professionals, she still found it possible to believe that her health could be restored. What was the basis for her remarkable faith?

Matthew gives us a revealing insight when he notes that "she kept saying to herself, 'if I can only touch his coat, I will get well'" (Mt 9:21 Williams). She confronted her fears and doubts by telling herself repeatedly that she still had reason for hope—her past did not have to define her future.

Talking to Ourselves
Psychologists today would say that this woman benefited from positive "self-talk." The term has emerged in recent decades, both in pop psychology and in more serious psychological circles as well, to describe an important part of our mechanism of thinking. Enthusiasts note that much—if not most—of our thinking is *verbalized*. If I wake up in the morning feeling depressed about the day ahead, for instance, I'm not just feeling some vague sense of despondency but am actually verbalizing a negative message to myself, such as, "I haven't had enough sleep. I won't be able to cope with the pressures ahead of me today, and I know the boss is going to give me too much to do." When we stop and look carefully at what is going on in our minds, we find that we're constantly talking to ourselves for good or ill during every conscious moment of life.

It is noted, too, that we can fall into certain patterns of negative self-talk early in life which if not checked continue with us for a lifetime. We are endlessly verbalizing messages to ourselves—consciously and unconsciously—about our prospects for success and happiness, and these mental memorandums dramatically affect our destiny. Persons with chronically low self-esteem, for instance, are constantly uttering statements of disapproval to themselves, such as, "I am no good. I make a mess of everything I try to do. I don't really have the right stuff to make friends or be successful, and even if I make the effort, no one is going to like me anyway."

Proponents of self-talk therapy argue that we can change virtually any behavior or thought pattern merely by altering the messages we speak to ourselves—"reprogramming the tracks," as it's called. To improve your self-image, for instance, simply make a habit of telling yourself, *I am someone of profound worth. I have the ability to make good friends and keep them and the potential to make a significant mark in this world.* Or, if you're frightened about an upcoming job interview, calm your nerves and increase your prospects for success by saying repeatedly to yourself, *I have skills which are really needed by this company and have good reason to hope that the employer will quickly see this. I'll be calm, articulate and friendly and present my case convincingly.*

The most provocative claim of self-talk devotees is that such efforts at constructive self-talk can quickly bring significant results and that they hold the key to personal change—even to spiritual growth. In one of the most popular and influential books on the subject, *The Self-Talk Solution,* Shad Helmstetter regards positive self-talk as having a virtually hypnotic effect on our psyche. Simply change the way you talk to yourself in a given area and surprising improvement will soon begin to take place, he insists. You can count on it.[1]

I Feel Good, I Feel Great . . .
Most of us react to such an idea with mixed emotions. We don't

deny that much of our thinking is verbalized (how could anyone argue with that?), and we suspect that there probably are benefits to working on our self-talk. Yet we balk at the notion that self-talk is a cure-all for our problems or an instant guarantee of health, happiness and success. For one thing, it's hard to rid ourselves of the thought that our efforts at positive self-talk easily amount to a glorified sort of wishful thinking.

I've never forgotten an Archie comic strip I once read and its lighthearted jab at positive thinking. As I recall it, Jughead tells Archie that he fears he will fail at something he wants to do. Archie then gives Jughead some time-honored advice: "Tell yourself you can do it. Speak positive messages of success to yourself."

Jughead answers, "That won't work. I know what a liar I am!"

The insight of that simple four-frame comic strip is actually astounding, for it highlights a major reason why efforts at positive thinking so often backfire for the person with low self-confidence—the fact that she mistrusts her own judgment to begin with! While she has plenty of dreams of success and happiness, she assumes that these are largely fantasy. A more confident counselor may encourage a person to verbalize positive messages to himself. Yet it does little good to tell himself repeatedly, "You'll be successful in this job interview," if a louder voice underneath keeps announcing, "You usually fail—and this attempt to psych yourself up is a delusion." His chances for success are about as good as those of multiphobic Bob in the movie *What About Bob?* who begins his daily routine and the movie chanting, "I feel good, I feel great, I feel wonderful," yet a moment later collapses in anxiety on the sidewalk.

Those with high self-esteem may benefit more readily from working on their self-talk. Yet they, too, likely discover that deeply ingrained thought patterns don't roll over and play dead as quickly as they would hope. It has been estimated that by the time we reach thirty years of age our brain has been subjected to three trillion mental impressions. It takes more than a few casual efforts at positive self-talk to reprogram such tracks!

But then there is the example of the woman with the hemorrhage. She clearly benefited from telling herself that she would be healed if she touched Jesus' robe. Her self-talk seems to be the factor that nudged her beyond a considerable barrier of fear. Her step of courage so impressed Jesus that he declared, "Daughter, your faith has made you well"—one of the handful of instances in the Gospels where he praised someone's faith (Mk 5:34). Her inspiring example brings us back to the fact that the Scriptures do see significance in the way we talk to ourselves.

What, then, are the real benefits of working on our self-talk, and what are the limitations?

Self-Talk in Scripture

To begin with—and for what it's worth—the Scriptures do give broad and perhaps surprising support to the fact that much of our thinking is verbalized. It's common, for instance, for biblical writers who are describing what an individual is thinking to use the words "said to himself." The phrase occurs frequently in Scripture and clues us to numerous examples of verbalized thinking in the Bible. Most of these fall well short of the redemptive example of self-talk displayed by the woman with the hemorrhage; many, in fact, underline just how misguided self-talk can often be. For instance:

• "Abraham fell facedown; he laughed and *said to himself,* 'Will a son be born to a man a hundred years old? Will Sarah bear a child at the age of ninety?'" (Gen 17:17).

• "[The wicked man] *says to himself,* 'God has forgotten; he covers his face and never sees'" (Ps 10:11).

• "This is the carefree city that lived in safety. She *said to herself,* 'I am, and there is none besides me'" (Zeph 2:15).

• "But suppose that servant is wicked and *says to himself,* 'My master is staying away a long time,' and he then begins to beat his fellow servants and to eat and drink with drunkards" (Mt 24:48-49).

Although these examples and many like them are negative, they do show that Scripture respects the fact that we verbalize our thinking. They bring out, too, that our self-talk has more than a trivial effect upon our destiny.

There are also clear exhortations in Scripture to work on our self-talk. For example:

• "After the LORD your God has driven them out before you, *do not say to yourself,* 'The LORD has brought me here to take possession of this land because of my righteousness'" (Deut 9:4).

• *"Fix these words of mine in your hearts and minds;* tie them as symbols on your hands and bind them on your foreheads. Teach them to your children, talking about them when you sit at home and when you walk along the road, when you lie down and when you get up" (Deut 11:18-19).

These commands exhort us to constantly express to ourselves and others a grace-centered perspective on God. The fact that we're commanded to do this is encouraging to consider, for it indicates that God has given us the ability to do what is commanded. We *can* make improvements in our self-talk, in other words: Scripture *does* give us hope at this point.

No Quick Fix

Scripture, however, never comes close to suggesting that our lives can be dramatically improved or that deep-seated habits of thinking can be quickly changed merely by focusing on our self-talk alone. While the Bible is highly optimistic about the possibility of positive change occurring in our lives, it cautions us against any attempt at a quick fix.

This comes across vividly in a discussion which Jesus had with his disciples about faith. On one occasion they came to him with an understandable request, "Increase our faith!" (Lk 17:5). Undoubtedly they were envious of Jesus' remarkable thought control. They wanted his uncanny capacity to believe without wavering that someone would be healed on command or—may we speculate?—that needs in their own lives would be instantly met. They wanted to get rid of all those negative messages inside their heads which kept saying, "This is impossible."

Jesus replied, "If you have faith as small as a mustard seed, you can say to this mulberry tree, 'Be uprooted and planted in the sea,' and it will obey you" (Lk 17:6). At first his reply seems puzzling, for he merely spoke to them of the challenge of increasing their faith, not about *how* to do it. He didn't seem to answer the question they asked. Yet I suspect Jesus realized that his disciples were looking for an easy shortcut to faith. He meant his response as a reality check, to jolt them into realizing the extreme difficulty of what they were asking. Even a very small *genuine* change in perspective is radical in nature and far-reaching in its effects. Or to say it conversely, it takes more than a few efforts at thought control or a wave of a spiritual magic wand to bring about an authentic change in outlook. This requires nothing less than a true inner transformation—and that takes time.

The point is pertinent to our discussion on self-talk, for our concern in improving our self-talk is, after all, how to increase our faith. Here we are reminded that our greatest faith need is not to become momentarily psyched up but to experience a thoroughgoing change in perspective. We need to become *thoroughly persuaded* of Christ's vibrant outlook on our life, not just temporarily enthused about it.

This brings us back, then, to the question of how such a radical change in perspective can come about.

Temporary Elation vs. True Transformation

A variety of steps may be helpful, including regular worship, careful study of Scripture, seeking the support and encouragement of others—even professional counseling if needed. Yet over the long haul, I do not believe that any activity helps us more to gain an outlook of faith than times of personal meditation. By "meditation" I don't mean incantations or lotus postures but simply a time of quiet pondering, when we reflect on our life and on God, and when we give Christ an ample opportunity to get our ear. It's through such periods that the most substantial and lasting changes in perspective are likely to occur.

This is the lesson we learn from Psalm 73. The writer of that psalm was overwhelmed with bitterness as he compared his lot in life to that of certain unscrupulous individuals he knew who were outrageously successful. He concluded that God had dealt him a low blow. Yet through a period of silent reflection he began to recognize the fate of these fraudulent individuals more clearly and to view his own life more optimistically. He moved beyond his acid spirit of comparison to a more vibrant outlook on God—and on his own life as well.

For him, the change in perspective occurred in the reverent stillness of a sanctuary. There was nothing magic about that location, for Moses had similar experiences on a mountain, Jesus in a garden, while John the Baptist and Paul benefited from the peaceful environment of the desert. The location is not the critical factor, as Jesus indicated when he suggested that we pray in a "closet" (Mt 6:6 KJV). The important matter is simply to arrange for a reasonable period of quiet and to choose a location which will enhance that.

I believe that each of us will benefit greatly from spending at least a few minutes daily in quiet reflection. During this period we should bring to the surface those areas of our life where we feel frustrated or discouraged. We should consider the hidden benefits which these situations may actually have for us and leisurely explore possible solutions and reasons for hope. We should ponder the biblical teaching on Christ's grace and provision in our lives and consider what relation this teaching has to the challenges we're facing. God has made our minds amazingly resilient, incredibly capable of regaining a sense of hope and generating optimistic solutions. Yet for this to happen we have to allow adequate opportunity for the Holy Spirit to influence us and renew within us the mind of Christ. This means especially the need for times of quiet.

Ideally this meditation should occur during a regular devotional time, when we pray and study Scripture as well as take time to reflect. Unfortunately our "quiet" times too often become cluttered with busy routines—prayer lists, study requirements and other rituals, which can become a subtle effort to court God's favor through our spirituality. While these practices can be valuable, we must remember that the ultimate purpose of a devotional time is to give praise to Christ and to gain his perspective and encouragement for our day. George Muller expressed it well when he said, "I consider it my first business of the day to get my heart happy in the Lord." Each of us needs to experiment to find out what approach will best accomplish that purpose. Most of us will find that a period of quiet, uncluttered reflection will be immensely helpful, even if it means discarding some of the busy routine of our devotional time.

Early in his career, Christian psychiatrist Paul Tournier decided to devote an hour daily to this sort of meditation. His many books bustle with stories of how this practice benefited both himself and his patients. Though setting this hour aside meant cutting back on other responsibilities, Tournier insists that the tradeoff was more than worth it.

An hour daily of personal meditation may be too much for some of us. Yet each of us will find that *some* time given each day to such reflection will benefit us and be worth the exchange of time involved. From time to time we will also find that a personal retreat or special extended period of prayer and reflection will help greatly to clarify things and rekindle our faith.

More Than Just Talk

Let's return to the example of the woman with the hemorrhage. I believe that her extraordinary faith sprang not merely from efforts to psych herself up but from a deep conviction about the grace and goodness of God. In spite of her extreme suffering, she was profoundly persuaded that God desired the very best for her and that she had considerable reason for hope. Her illness, in fact, may well have provided the enforced solitude for her to think things through to this point. As she ventured forth to seek healing from Jesus, she was dreadfully frightened—and naturally so, for she had plenty of inertia to overcome, the reactions of unsympathetic people to face and plenty of disheartening thoughts to deal with. In light of this, telling herself again and again that Jesus could heal her did prove helpful—but in reality *she was simply reminding herself of what she already knew.*

Here we finally come to the point of saying what is the real benefit of working on our self-talk. *Self-talk has maintenance value for us.* It's a way of bringing ourselves back to points of conviction we've already reached during times of quiet reflection before the Lord, especially as the more frantic pace of life drowns them out. It's a way of combating fears that all too naturally crop up, even once we become convinced of what God wants us to do. When used in healthy balance with times of prayer and meditation, it can truly aid us in practicing the presence of the Lord.

You and I need to keep telling ourselves that.

9

Contagious Optimism

When the Sons of Thunder was close to disbanding, it faced a financial crisis. During the previous year this Christian musical group which I directed had accumulated a debt of $5,000. Though that doesn't sound like much by today's standards, to us young folks in 1974 it might as well have been $5,000,000. We wracked our brains in band meetings but couldn't figure any way out short of bankruptcy.

Things changed dramatically when a friend with a gift for thinking optimistically came and gave us a pep talk. While he didn't offer any specific solution, he said that he was certain we had the resources to solve this problem. He knew there were steps we could take to do it.

That was both a comforting and challenging thought, and it took well with us. Our discussions took on a more positive tone after that, and within a short time we arrived at a plan: We would invite former band members to join us for a farewell-reunion concert and sell tickets. In addition, we would let concerned friends know of our need, hoping some would help with donations. Though only two months remained to pull these details together, we felt determined to give it our best.

The Lord blessed our efforts immensely. The concert was surprisingly successful, contributions came in, and in the end we raised almost exactly the amount needed to pay off our debt. While there were many miracles to celebrate, the greatest was that God through one optimistic friend got us thinking hopefully about our situation. We had practically convinced ourselves that our predicament had no solution. Once we began thinking constructively, an answer quickly came.

I had a similar experience several years later, when I again benefited from the optimism of a positive-thinking friend. Our family was living in a townhouse, and my office was in the basement. Because an open stairway connected the basement and the first floor, I was often distracted by noise from upstairs. The obvious solution would be to install a door. Yet since the stairway had an open, expansive design, I couldn't think of any logical way to fit a door into the wide space at the top or bottom of the stairs. I'm embarrassed to admit how much time I spent mulling the problem over, trying to come up with a workable design. I concluded there was no solution short of a major modification to the stairway (which would violate the community's architectural standards and be too expensive to undertake).

One evening, though, I shared my dilemma at a Bible study. A man whom I respected for his constructive approach to problems responded that he was sure there would be an easy way to install a door. His confidence inspired me, and I thought, *He's right, there must be a way to do it.* The next day it dawned on me that I could insert a door at the landing point where the stairway turned halfway down; since the stairwell was more enclosed there, this was an easy modification to make.

The solution was, in fact, so obvious and simple that I couldn't believe I hadn't thought of it before. I had been locked into thinking that a door would have to be placed at the top or bottom of the staircase. Only when I began thinking optimistically did it occur to me that there was another alternative—to install it in the middle. And this was the solution that worked.

Optimism and Faith

It may not seem profound to say that our attitude affects our approach to challenges. In a general way we all recognize this to be true. Yet most of the time we fall to appreciate the *extent* to which this is true. Our pessimism can literally shut down our creative energy for solving a problem. Even worse, it channels that energy in the wrong direction. When a problem seems difficult, we can be incredibly clever at convincing ourselves it has no solution. Once we reach that conclusion, we interpret all the evidence we see as proof that we're correct—the problem is indeed beyond hope. Having established that fact, we can overlook obvious solutions which may be staring us in the face.

When we are able to make that extraordinary shift to thinking optimistically, however, it's remarkable how quickly we sometimes find a way to remedy our predicament. In some cases we're astonished at how obvious the solution actually is.

Yet reaching this point of optimism can be no small challenge. When faced with a difficult problem, we can fall into a pessimistic manner of thinking about it, often without realizing this is happening.

My experiences particularly bring to mind how others' attitudes affect our own. We are creatures of suggestion, and we easily and unconsciously absorb the positive or negative outlook of those around us.

We see examples of both types of influence occurring throughout Scripture. It's interesting, for instance, how frequently in Scripture individuals manage to convince one another that a situation is hopeless even though God sees it in a positive light. The spies whom Moses sent to Canaan are a classic example of how this negative "groupthink" occurs. Even though God had promised that Israel would conquer Canaan (Num 13:1), ten of the twelve spies sent to investigate the land concluded that the obstacles to success were simply too great. We sense that these men, as brilliant as they were, used their intelligence to convince each other that the mission would be too difficult for them. In effect they talked themselves out of faith.

A similar example is the occasion when Jesus' disciples were in a boat with him, desperately concerned about where their next meal was coming from. Mark notes that they discussed the fact that they had no bread, and Jesus then upbraided them for their lack of faith (Mk 8:16-21). What is striking is that the disciples actually did have a loaf of bread with them (v. 14); even more astounding is that they had helped Jesus feed a crowd of thousands with only a few loaves and fish earlier that same day. They failed, though, to notice the one loaf they had in the boat—let alone to consider what the power of Jesus could do to multiply it. Their discussion only served to strengthen their pessimism about his capacity to meet their needs.

While examples like these abound in Scripture, there are many positive ones as well, where one person's optimism inspires another's. One of my favorites is the story of Lamech and Noah. Genesis records only one significant fact about Lamech, Noah's father: after Noah's birth, he declared, "[Noah] will comfort us in the labor and painful toil of our hands caused by the ground the LORD has cursed" (Gen 5:29). Since this is the one notable detail the Holy Spirit chose to record about Lamech, I assume it describes his prevailing attitude toward his son. Lamech apparently had an exceptionally high level of confidence in Noah's integrity and creative ability. He undoubtedly was one who constantly told his son, "You can do it!"

Whatever else we conclude about Noah, he was clearly a skilled problem solver. His creative ingenuity was remarkable. The logistical complexities of building the ark and organizing its mission would have been monumental. While God gave Noah many instructions, there is no evidence that he directly revealed to him all the details of the project. It appears, rather, that he left Noah with many problems to resolve on his own. Yet all of the evidence suggests that he successfully tackled each of these challenges and never concluded that any was too difficult.

Noah certainly benefited from his father's high expectations of him. Lamech's conviction that his son would make a difference helped give Noah the courage to tackle problems which most would have thought insurmountable.

Positive Influences

The lesson is clear: we desperately need the influence of optimistic people in our lives. In my own life there have been so many instances like the two I've mentioned, where a single individual inspired me to think hopefully about a situation which I thought was at a dead end. While that person may not have given me a solution to my problem, he or she inspired enough optimism that I was able to open my eyes and see a solution.

We need to accept how vastly influential the power of suggestion is in our lives. As Paul Tournier points out in his classic book *The Person Reborn,* our suggestibility is not in itself a weakness but is part of the humanity God has put within us. Our need, Tournier notes, is not to avoid situations which affect our suggestible nature but to place ourselves in those situations where the most redemptive "suggestions" occur.[1] This is a vital point to keep in mind as we plan our activities with people.

Each of us will benefit greatly from having at least one friend who is a supreme optimist, who believes the best for us and has a special knack for encouraging us when our world looks bleak. If we don't have such a friendship, we should pray earnestly that Christ will provide it, and we should take what steps we can to find it. If we have the good fortune to gain such a friend, we should give high priority to spending time with this person and benefiting from his or her positive outlook.

In addition, we should take advantage of the affirmation that comes through more indirect means, such as books, articles, teachers, preachers and—yes—even media personalities.

Last but far from least, we need to structure our daily devotional time in a way that allows Christ to breathe his optimism and encouragement into our lives. Yes, we need to study the whole of Scripture and focus on both the love and justice of God. Yet we should give emphasis to the triumphant themes of Scripture: God's grace, which is greater than our sin; his adequacy, which is more powerful than our inadequacy; his guidance, which overrules our confusion and waywardness. Again, it helps to spend time in silent reflection, dwelling on God's goodness and recounting his blessings in our lives. It is worth letting more busy aspects of our quiet time go in order for this to happen.

Each of us needs a heavy and frequent dose of optimism. Keeping our hearts cheerful and hopeful is not just good stress management but foundational to faith in Christ. I'm certain it's a vital part of the good soil which Christ speaks of in the parable of the sower, which gives harvest to the seed of faith (Mt 13:3-9).

We must simply keep in mind the role others play in keeping the soil fertile. Here the truth of the ancient adage always applies: "Choose your friends wisely."

IV

Miracles Come in Many Forms

10

A Matter of Timing

One morning recently, volunteers from a local shelter stopped by our home to pick up a bed we were donating to their mission. The driver backed his truck up our steep driveway and stopped at the top where we had left the bed for them. I walked outside, spoke with the men briefly, then went back in the house. After quickly loading the bed in the truck, they climbed back in and began to drive away. By now I had walked to the bedroom in the rear of our home.

Suddenly I heard a crackling noise like a small thunderclap, and our house went dark. I instantly feared the worst.

I rushed to the living room window, and my fears were confirmed. I could see the overhead power lines which feed into our one-story home draped over the truck, now stopped at the end of our driveway. Its trailer had snagged these low-hanging wires and pulled them loose from the side of our house.

Immediately I panicked and began to imagine a number of imminent disasters. The men in the truck were in danger of electrocution if they stepped out of the cab. If these live wires dropped to the ground, they would charge our front yard with high voltage, endangering anyone coming near our home. It could be hours—or days!—until the power company came to make repairs. Meanwhile I'd have to keep watch and warn children and other unsuspecting souls not to touch the exposed lines.

My heart sank, for I had much to do that day, and here I was stuck with this obstruction in the driveway, making it impossible for me to leave. I couldn't even phone for help, since the truck had ripped down the phone lines as well.

The men in the truck, however, could see things from a different perspective. The driver stepped out of his cab and walked up the street. Fortunately the exposed wires dangling near the truck were not actually touching its metal, so he wasn't harmed. I assumed he had gone to make a phone call and carefully walked out into the driveway to await the news. He returned quickly and assured me that help was on the way—immediately.

He explained that service personnel from Potomac Edison, the power company in our area, were working just up the street, trimming tree limbs off of power lines. A minute later their cherry-picker pulled up in front of our house, and more men in yellow hard hats than I could count jumped out and descended on our yard. Within a short time the severed wires were reconnected, and the phone line as well. Lights came back on, the men from the power company drove away and the mission workers left. It was as though nothing had happened—like a scene out of *Cat in the Hat.*

I was left dumbfounded, wondering at the sheer unlikelihood of technicians from Potomac Edison being nearby at such a moment of crisis. What is the probability of that? Infinitesimal at best.

Time on Our Side

Yet God is not bound by probability. Or as Albert Einstein put it, "God doesn't play dice." He exercises providential oversight in our lives which vastly exceeds our awareness.

And his timing is never off. It's the exquisite timing of God which most intrigues me as I reflect on this incident. The power company squad was there at exactly the moment I needed them, in spite of the extreme odds against it. The incident was admittedly unusual. Yet I believe that from time to time God gives us experiences like this as a window on his broader and more mysterious work in our lives. He wants us to know that his timing is always perfect, in every aspect of our experience.

We instinctively mistrust the timing of God, and this lack of trust accounts for much of our anxiety Yet a close look at our experience shows how flawless his timing actually is. With the benefit of hindsight, we often recognize how remarkably advantageous his timing has been in the events of our lives.

Scripture constantly extols the timing of God. Since I write this chapter at the Christmas season, my attention is drawn particularly to the events surrounding Christ's birth. No portion of biblical history seems to better highlight the majesty and perfection of God's timing. Jesus was born in the "fullness of the time," Paul declares (Gal 4:4 KJV). The convergence of human events was perfectly orchestrated for his entrance.

We now recognize a multitude of ways in which this was true. Christian historian Kenneth Scott Latourette notes, "Jesus was born in the reign of Augustus. After a long period of wars which had racked the Mediterranean and its shores, political unity had been achieved. . . . Never before had all the shores of the Mediterranean been under one rule and never had they enjoyed such prosperity."[1] The benefits of this time of cooperation included a unified language and an elaborate road system that provided unprecedented ease of travel. Yet the urbanization which resulted left many feeling disoriented, fostering a hunger for spiritual perspective which the Christian gospel answered.

It's clear now that God knew exactly what he was doing in bringing Christ to earth when he did. While this is interesting from the standpoint of history, it also has profound implications for us who follow Christ. We can take comfort in knowing that the same power of timing which affected the events of Christ's birth also operates in the circumstances of our individual lives. God's ways with Christ were meant, in part, to show his ways with us (Rom 8:11, 32).

Setting Our Clocks

While there is great encouragement in knowing this, there is a significant challenge as well. When I reflect on the first Christmas, I'm often stunned to think that very few people—only a handful— were at all aware that anything extraordinary was taking place. For the vast majority of the people of that time it was simply business as usual.

It takes spiritual alertness to appreciate the timing of God. And to respond to it. God graciously allows us to experience the benefits of his timing in countless ways, even when we're not consciously trying to cooperate with him. He works behind the scenes in untold ways to protect us and provide for us. Yet within certain boundaries he also gives us freedom to make decisions which do or do not conform with his timing. Here, though, the challenge comes in understanding his timing. There is no easy formula for doing this, and we should not be too quick to think we grasp his plans. He has radically different clocks for each of us. Consider examples from the Christmas story:

• *A woman past the childbearing years gives birth to a son.* How often we give up too early on a personal goal and let failure convince us God has said no, when in reality he has simply said "Wait."

• *A very young woman conceives a child miraculously.* Sometimes God is ready for us to move ahead before we think it is logical to do so.

• *Mary gives birth to Jesus in the humble setting of a stable.* We can think we're unprepared to do something because we lack certain material benefits. In fact, these may not be at all necessary to carry out what Christ wants us to do.

And with a number of those in the Christmas story we observe something intriguing: *They were simply going about their routine responsibilities when God intervened and gave them a role in the events surrounding Christ's birth.*

When we look closely at those privileged few who participated in the first Christmas, it seems that they not only had a heart for God but a unique bent for *listening* to him. There were Zechariah, Anna and Simeon, who prayed regularly in the temple. Mary and Elizabeth also gave earnest attention to prayer. There were the wise men, who undoubtedly spent much time seeking God. Then there were the shepherds, who were watching their flocks in the field when the angel confronted them. While we don't know whether or not they were praying at that time, their vocation allowed them considerable time for quiet reflection. God had the chance to get their attention.

The message, then, is clear: If I am to enjoy the benefits of God's timing in my life, I need to give to him something for which there is no other substitute: *time*. It is perhaps the greatest irony of the Christmas season that we become so busy at this time of year that we have less time than ever to be still before the Lord. Again we come back to the fact that our greatest spiritual need is to set aside time for being alone with Christ and seeking his perspective. Resolve to spend at least a few minutes each day privately with Christ, listening to him and giving him the opportunity to guide your decisions.

While God's timing in our lives will always remain a mystery, the secret to keeping in pace with it is not. Give him the time he needs to get your ear and to impress on you his direction for your life.

11

Bailing Us Out

Halfway *through an intensive graduate program I lost my* zeal. My pastoral heartstrings tugged at me; I wanted to get out of academia and back into people-centered ministry. I came close to quitting.

On Evie's advice I decided to seek counsel from the dean of students. When I walked into his office the next morning, he received me warmly and spoke with me at length, even though I hadn't made an appointment. After I explained my dilemma, he offered some simple advice: Since I'd come this far in the program, it was a minimal sacrifice to continue. Besides, the long-range benefits of finishing the degree well outweighed the momentary relief of getting out.

Fortunately his counsel hit a receptive chord, and his affirming spirit was reassuring. By the end of our meeting my motivation had begun to return. I'm now eternally grateful to this man for his advice and encouragement. Staying with the program gave me the background to write my first book, and the degree has opened numerous doors of ministry. In this case God used a man—one individual—to keep me from a regrettable course of action. Were it not for his counsel, I likely would have bailed out

The experience speaks to me of God's protective hand in my life. As I reflect on his protection, I'm reminded not only of individuals who have been like angels of light to me but of fortuitous circumstances, like the power company's presence in our neighborhood just when I needed them. Remembering such moments of protection always reinforces my faith.

One evening when we were living in St. Louis, I was studying in my basement office. I took a short break to go to the kitchen for a soda and while upstairs heard the noise of glass shattering in the basement. I rushed downstairs to find that the fluorescent bulb over my desk had come loose, falling onto my desk and exploding into hundreds of fragments. I had barely missed being in its range of fire.

The "barely missed" scenario describes more than a few experiences I've had with automobiles. Since I spend considerable time driving—often to retreats in remote locations—I worry about having a flat tire. *Will I be able pry loose those intractable lug nuts that are blasted tight by an air gun? And what if I'm on my way to a speaking engagement—how will I clean up after making the repair?* During the 170,000 miles that we drove our previous car before recently trading it in, a tire blew out only once. It happened just as I was pulling up to the home of two husky friends, who quickly emerged from the house and changed the tire for me.

Rescue Missions

I'm not building up to the idea that the Christian never experiences problems or that faith will deliver us from every predicament. God allows challenge and pain to come into our lives as needed to strengthen us and increase our dependency on him.

Yet a friend and I agreed in a recent conversation that our most common experience of God's grace has been of his providing ways out of tight spots. Often these have been predicaments of our own making—dilemmas into which our limited insight has plunged us. Call this a rescue operation if you will. I'm perfectly comfortable with the idea. In fact, if we don't have a profound and ongoing sense of *needing* to be rescued, we will miss many of the benefits of the grace of God.

But this sense of need must be accompanied by the conviction that God will come to our rescue. We need this confidence not only for the sake of humility (as vital as that is) but for the sake of *courage.* One of the reasons we hesitate to take important steps of faith—toward building relationships or seeking better opportunities for our gifts—is our fear of problems that might confront us on the way.

Divine Compensation

Throughout his earthly ministry Jesus demonstrated his willingness to care for those who followed him, to the point of bailing them out of the most hideous predicaments. His first miracle, in fact, was precisely such a rescue mission. He and his disciples were attending a wedding feast in Cana (Jn 2:1-11). Marriage celebrations in New Testament times amounted to festivals that lasted for many days. The families of the bride and groom were often bound by a legal contract, and the groom's family could be sued if the reception's provisions were inadequate. Partway through this particular feast, the wine gave out. Jesus proceeded to transform the water filling six twenty-gallon jugs into wine of superb quality.

By changing water into the very best wine, Jesus not only taught a symbolic truth about the superiority of the new covenant over the old. He also demonstrated something profoundly practical about God's willingness to come to our aid in human affairs. By protecting the groom's family from embarrassment and legal liability, he showed how God can shield us from unforeseen consequences as we take steps of faith.

Jesus showed his willingness to rescue us in perhaps an even

more comforting way through his last miracle—restoring the ear of
the high priest's servant after Peter slashed it off (Jn 18:10-11; Lk
22:50-51). Peter undoubtedly intended to do something far more
destructive with his sword—to kill the servant or the high priest
himself. The healing of the servant's ear not only symbolizes God's
rectifying our mistakes but reminds us that he often protects us from
the more extreme effects of our impulsive and destructive tendencies.

A Confident Perspective

We should meditate often on the fact of God's rescue missions in
our lives, for this is one of the vital ways in which he shows his
providential care for us. Appreciating his willingness to rescue us
shouldn't lead to sloppiness in our walk with Christ ("If God will
bail me out, I can do whatever I want"). If it does, then we haven't
taken the grace of God seriously to begin with! To the contrary, it
should strengthen our boldness to take steps of faith.

I realize it can sometimes be hard to know precisely *what* God
wants us to do. We may struggle long and hard to discern his will
for a particular decision. Yet even as we come to understand it,
we're often panicked at the thought of moving forward. Our mind
is filled with countless "what ifs"—imagined future disasters which
paralyze us from taking action. At this time especially we need to
be fortified by confidence in God's willingness to rescue us if it
proves necessary.

From the human angle, of course, we want to figure out solutions to all potential problems before they arise. Yet concern with
troubleshooting every possible contingency in advance will paralyze us from ever taking a major step of faith. As the Cana wedding
feast reminds us, the time comes when we simply need to move
ahead, trusting that God is abundantly able to come to our rescue
when our planning has been inadequate. And as he protected Peter
in the incident with the servant's ear, he can safeguard us from the
effects of our more extreme human tendencies.

God cannot steer a parked car. But as we move forward, we discover his infinite ability to navigate our lives. And he is just as able to do the maintenance necessary to keep us on course.

12

Rumors
of Miracles

*I*n The Road Less Traveled, *M. Scott Peck writes of his fascina-*
tion with "serendipities." These are special but inexplicable experiences of blessing. Events occur in our lives, he notes, which bring
great benefit yet defy logical explanation. The personal experiences
I related in the last two chapters would be examples of serendipity.
Yet Peck does not hesitate to term such incidents *miracles.*[1]

Peck marvels, for instance, at how sometimes in a dreadful traffic
accident an individual will emerge from a mangled vehicle un-
harmed. This seems to point to the miraculous protection of God.

Peck speaks with no less intrigue of a fortunate experience he
had while working on his book. Having some unexpected time during a trip, he retired to a colleague's study to write. Writer's block
struck, though, and Peck couldn't resolve how to proceed with the
chapter he was drafting. As he sat befuddled, his friend's wife walked
in carrying a book she wanted to share with him. The book that she
lent to him provided exactly the insight he needed, and he was able
to move ahead with his writing. Again, serendipity was the only

word to describe the experience.

The serendipitous events Peck notes are not unique. We each have had experiences like these, perhaps many of them. Yet typically we think of them not as miracles but fortuitous coincidences. In fact, Peck claims, we may be witnessing the supernatural intervention of God more frequently than we realize.

What makes Peck's perspective so interesting is that he was not a Christian when he arrived at it. Though he became a believer shortly after publishing *The Road Less Traveled,* he wrote the book simply as an observer of human life and not with a particular theological stance to promote. When he looked honestly at his own experience and that of others, he concluded that there was a miraculous element present at times which couldn't be ignored.

I find Peck's viewpoint refreshing, for it suggests that even without the benefit of biblical revelation, there is plenty in ordinary experience to convince us of the reality of miracles, if we'll open our eyes to the evidence. To the thinking person, in fact, it is more logical to look upon certain fortuitous events as miracles than to write them off as coincidences. His observations inspire us to be more alert to God's uncanny protection and provision in our lives.

Bending the Rules

It's hard to read the Bible and not conclude that our belief in the possibility of miracles needs to be very strong. It's a basic theme of Scripture that the God who created the rules of nature can overrule them if he wishes. And it's a pervasive theme, for examples of God's doing exactly that abound throughout his Word.

It's hard, also, to read the Bible and not conclude that our view of what *constitutes* a miracle needs expanding. Consider the fact that Jesus referred to his miracles as "works." After healing a man born blind, for instance, he declared to his disciples, "We must work the works of him who sent me, while it is day" (Jn 9:4 RSV). The miracle in this case was Jesus' most impressive one next to raising Lazarus, for while Jewish history had accounts of blind persons regaining their sight, there was no record of anyone blind from birth being healed. This was a miracle of miracles to the people of Jesus' time. Yet Jesus referred to it merely as a "work." It was part of the *ordinary* activity of God, in other words, not the extraordinary.[2]

Jesus was saying that for God to perform a miracle is simply business as usual. It's part of his normal function in managing human life.

On the other hand, Jesus' language prods us to see the extraordinary in the ordinary events of life. It inspires us to think more creatively about what happens to us and to realize that in many cases it is more reverent—and accurate—to regard fortuitous coincidences as miracles of God.

Perhaps another way to say it is this: While a miracle involves God's bending the rules, these "rules" are not only those of physical nature but of other areas of life as well. They may involve the following:

- the rules of economics (God enables me to sell my home even though "no one's buying")
- the rules of employment (he enables me to find a job even though "no one's hiring")
- the rules of education (he enables me to get through a course I thought would be too difficult to finish)
- the rules of inspiration (he enables me to write a paper I thought would be impossible for me)
- the rules of relationships (he brings reconciliation with someone with whom I had an "irreconcilable difference")
- the rules of romance (he enables me to find marriage at a point in life when it seemed inconceivable)
- the rules of psychological stamina (he gives me strength for a trial which I thought I could never endure)

It's helpful to expand our concept of miracles to include serendipities such as these, for when they occur we are quicker to recognize God's power at work. And as our conviction that God is willing to perform miracles grows, we are more alert to the practical ways he may work in our lives.

Faith vs. Presumption

This isn't to say that all belief in miracles is healthy. There is an important distinction—and a thin line sometimes—between reverent respect for God's ability to perform miracles and presumptuous expectation that they will occur. Generally, if my expectation of miracles is not accompanied by the willingness to obey Christ and live responsibly, and also by a humble recognition that I don't know God's intention for the future, then my "faith" is better termed presumption.

The compulsive gambler, for instance, who against all odds believes he will win the high stakes, has a strong belief in miracles. So does the person who refuses to work yet assumes that God will provide his needs. So does the intoxicated person cruising at eighty-five miles per hour who imagines that God will protect him. None of these people, though, comes close to displaying faith in the biblical sense.

While the Scriptures challenge us to a deeper conviction about miracles, they emphasize just as strongly our need to take responsibility, to be good stewards of our lives and to grow in our ability to solve problems. If there are obvious steps I can take toward meeting a need, I am presumptuous to expect God to provide for it in a more direct, miraculous way. I am likewise naive to expect him to shield me miraculously from the effects of reckless behavior. While he protects us in countless ways from unexpected problems that arise, we cannot expect him to come to our rescue if we deliberately court disaster.

By the same token, I am wrong to think that I ever know for certain that God will perform a given miracle or act in a particular way. The Scriptures remind us constantly that we cannot know the mind of God for our future, for such unbending certainty would remove the need for walking step by step in faith.

Having a general conviction that God is able and willing to perform miracles, though, is not presumptuous, if I'm not presuming to know how God will act and not banking on a miracle to bail me out of responsibility. Under these conditions believing in God's power to perform miracles will not lead me to be less responsible but *more so*. In some cases this belief will even give me the extra impetus needed to succeed.

Miracles and Motivation

No matter how carefully we think through a step of faith, no matter how thoroughly we pray about it, no matter how diligently we plan the details, we often reach a point where the challenge seems simply too great. The odds are stacked against us, we conclude, and failure is inevitable. Ironically, we are sometimes much closer to succeeding at this point than we realize, and one further effort makes all the difference. It's here that faith in God's ability to do miracles can be so critical, for without it we may lack the motivation to go ahead.

In my years of performing music with bands there were more than a few occasions when a fiasco occurred, prior to an event, that threatened to ruin our presentation. Yet when we went ahead and played, the performance came off well, in some cases remarkably so.

When I was only fourteen, a musical group I had formed was scheduled to play for a school function which we considered important. Yet as the date approached, three of the band's five members informed me that they wouldn't be able to participate. Panicked, I phoned around and found two very inexperienced high-school musicians—a saxophone player and a drummer—who were willing to join with the bass player and me to play the engagement. There was no time to rehearse, however; it would be a classic case of "winging it."

A big part of me wanted to phone the school and tell them we had to bow out. But even at that young age I felt compelled by that dogged sense that the show must go on.

I was terribly apprehensive when we walked on stage that evening, certain we would fall flat on our adolescent faces. Yet the audience was warm and receptive, and the substitute musicians were excited to be performing. The energy was somehow right, and though we made many mistakes that evening, the music had that unmistakable quality which can only be called "life." The audience responded well and did not seem the least bit aware that we were hanging together by a thread.

It's an experience I've never forgotten, and one which in various ways has been repeated many times in the years since then. If you perform music or act, you've probably had unnerving episodes like this. In spite of your best efforts to prepare, a problem arises which threatens disaster. Yet you go ahead anyway and then are wonderfully surprised by the results.

Most would simply credit such good fortune to "the magic of performing." Yet in some cases *miracle* is the better word for it. The obstacles to be overcome were simply too great to use a less inspired term to describe the outcome.

Going on stage in less than ideal circumstances is a helpful analogy to keep in mind for other challenges we face. In spite of our best preparations, we may feel that if we continue with a certain endeavor, we have as much chance for success as a soprano performing with laryngitis. Yet moving forward may be exactly what is needed to open ourselves to God's remarkable provision.

This "going on stage" may include
- finishing the course
- taking the exam
- completing the report
- applying for the job
- apologizing to the person we've offended
- making the investment
- phoning for the date
- giving the talk
- sharing Christ with the person who seems skeptical

Confidence in Christ's power to perform miracles can give us the push needed to take steps like these.

The Four Miracles

This confidence can come from reflecting on our own past experience of miracles and from meditating on the countless examples in Scripture. It helps, too, to think as broadly and creatively as possible about the various ways God brings about miracles, in order to be as open as possible to how he might work in our own lives. I've personally taken great heart from meditating on the different sorts of miracles pictured in the Bible. At least four major types are noted. They attest to the remarkable variety of ways Christ meets the "impossible" situations in people's lives.

1. The carte blanche miracle. This appears where Christ solves a problem instantaneously with virtually no effort required on a person's part. Most of the healing miracles pictured in the New Testament are of this type. Someone suffering the dire effects of a debilitating illness or deformity is relieved in an instant of the suffering. This isn't to say that no response was required from the person. In the majority of healing miracles it appears either that people made the effort to present themselves to Jesus and request healing or that someone else did this on their behalf. Yet beyond this basic step of faith they were passive, and the miracle resulted entirely from the benevolent action of Christ.

2. Abundance from meager provisions. A second type of miracle is shown in the two situations in the Gospels where Jesus feeds huge crowds of people with a few fish and loaves of bread. In these cases some human effort was involved—the providing of a small amount of food and the work of the disciples in organizing the crowd and distributing it. Yet the effort was minuscule compared to the provision made by Jesus.

These "miracles of expansion" give us hope not only for those impossible predicaments where there appears to be nothing we can do, but for the many situations where there is at least some small effort we can make. "God can do a lot with a little when he has all there is of it," as it is said. Yet so often we feel it just isn't worth the effort.

There's a wonderful message of encouragement here for those of us who preach or lead Bible studies. Even after careful preparation, we may feel as prepared to feed a group spiritually as the disciples did when they had to feed the enormous crowd with a handful of fish and loaves. We say, "Lord, there's no way I can do it!" Yet Christ is addressing us as he did his disciples, saying, *"You* give them something to eat" (Mk 6:37). If you're like me, you've often sensed that Christ's provision in a teaching situation has gone far beyond your preparations.

3. A sudden lift toward our goal. This third miracle is the one which intrigues me most. John records a time when Jesus' disciples make a valiant effort to row across a lake in the face of a difficult storm, with the winds against them (Jn 6:16-21). They have completed the greater part of their journey when Jesus suddenly appears, walking on the water. He steps into the boat and they are instantly at the shore!

In working on various projects I've sometimes had experiences which seem to parallel this incident. I've poured myself into an undertaking for some time, still expecting some major challenges, when through some unexpected serendipity the goal is suddenly reached.

Here the message seems to be that we shouldn't give up too easily. God honors our tenacity and perseverance. At any point he can give us sudden acceleration toward our goal.

4. Strength for the long haul. The fourth miracle is reflected in the words of God to the Israelites in Deuteronomy 29:5: "During the forty years that I led you through the desert, your clothes did not wear out, nor did the sandals on your feet." In certain situations, God chooses not to make things too easy for us. He allows us to run the full course toward reaching a goal. Yet the miracle is that our strength holds out, whereas we thought it wouldn't, and the provisions which we were certain would give out long before we reached our goal end up being sufficient. Certainly most of our experiences of going through college and other formal educational programs fit this pattern well!

We should meditate often not only on the fact of Christ's miracles but on the variety of those which he performs. Doing so will help keep us from the presumptuous spirit of thinking we know precisely how he will solve a problem, for we'll be reminded that he brings his grace to bear on our lives in a multitude of ways. Yet it will also keep us optimistic about receiving that grace and encourage us to take the steps necessary to receive his provision for our needs.

We can take heart, too, from the wonderful reminder that sometimes the answer to a pressing problem is only a step away.

13

The Availability Factor

When our son Ben announced last year that he was running for student council vice president, I thought, *What chance does he have to win as a fifth grader in this large elementary school with a number of sixth graders also vying for the spot? Yet* he waged a good campaign, and to our surprise and delight he won. This past month, on the strength of that gain, he ran for president and again was successful. I'm certain that there were other students at least as well qualified as Ben who would have liked to serve in these positions. Yet there was one critical difference: *Ben ran and they didn't.* He was optimistic enough to think he could win, and in the end his availability was the deciding factor.

I'm often intrigued with what a potent role our availability plays in what we accomplish. "Fifty percent of success is showing up," as it is said. This isn't to say that ability, potential and social skills are unimportant in success. Yet when we consider God's working in human life, it seems that he uses our availability at least as much as these other traits in opening doors.

This point is helpful to remember when we feel hesitant to take steps of faith. Because of inferiority or a sense of insignificance we may fail to knock on doors which actually would open to us. We're especially prone to hold back if we know that many others are available to meet a need or interested in the same goal we want to pursue. We assume that our efforts won't be as successful as theirs or that what we have to contribute isn't really needed.

In our modern, densely populated world it's all too easy to fall into such futility about life itself. What can I possibly do that will make a difference?

Three points are critical to keep in mind. One is that others often are not nearly as available for opportunities or as alert to them as we think. This point is shown in a surprising observation by sociologists. They note that someone with an emergency need in public is less likely to receive assistance if a crowd is present than if only a few people are nearby. The reason is that in a large group each person assumes that someone else will take responsibility—so no one does. The sense of individual accountability is greatly reduced. This explains those bizarre news stories we sometimes hear about someone being assaulted in front of a crowd while no one offers help. Merely making an anonymous phone call for help might have made the difference for the victim.

The second point is that God—again to cite the popular expression—can do a lot with a little when he has all there is of it. We noted that this principle is graphically demonstrated in the feeding miracles of the Gospels. In John's account of one of them, he mentions that a young boy actually made several fish and loaves available to Jesus to feed the crowd. Through his availability this boy helped feed a multitude of thousands. Of course, our hesitancy in the face of opportunity is often like Andrew's, who, when presenting the boy's provisions to Jesus, complained, "But what are they among so many?" (Jn 6:9 RSV). The incident reminds us, though, that Christ's power is manifested through our mere availability in ways that far transcend our potential or meager resources.

The third point is that God has put each of us on earth to accomplish certain purposes and carry out certain work for which *no one else is as well equipped.* As we carefully seek his direction, we can know that our efforts are distinctive and significant to the work Christ is doing in the world.

We may trust, then, that through our availability alone we are beginning from a position of strength in what we do. By being available we open ourselves to the miraculous working of Christ.

How It Applies

Let's consider further how the availability factor relates to several major areas of life.

Seeking opportunities to use our gifts. When looking for professional opportunities or other ways to employ our gifts, we easily become discouraged, thinking, "The best opportunities won't be open to me," or, "What can I do that others can't do just as well?" Yet the availability factor suggests that unmet opportunities may be far more plentiful than we think, and God's willingness to work through us at these points may be much greater than we realize.

Consider David's decision to fight Goliath. His conviction that he could tackle the giant sprang from recalling his success as a shepherd fighting wild animals with a sling (1 Sam 17:34-37). Since God's glory was now at stake, David assumed that God would give victory through this skill already so evident in his life. Yet thousands of Israelite soldiers had also been shepherds or hunters and had confronted ravenous animals just as David did. They had the identical basis for concluding that they could successfully battle Goliath. But none of them made this connection. *Not one.* David alone was able to see the situation with the eyes of faith.

David's example suggests that exceptional opportunities for using our gifts can exist which others simply don't recognize. We're given a basis for hope and optimism as we seek to realize our potential for Christ.

Seeking relationships. The availability factor also gives hope to those of us who are eager for a serious relationship or marriage. I speak with many singles in their twenties, thirties or beyond who fear that marriage has passed them by. "Anyone I'd want to marry is spoken for already," someone will say. Yet I'm convinced that the options for finding marriage are much greater than many realize.

Studies show, too, that most people end up marrying someone in close proximity to them. It may be a person with whom they work, attend school or come into contact frequently in church or another social setting. There is little basis for the notion that "absence makes the heart grow fonder." It is naive, too, to assume, "My prince/princess will come to my doorstep even though I make no effort to find this person." It is *proximity* that contributes to the growth of a relationship.

Understanding the role which proximity plays in relationships presents me with a challenge if I want to be married. It suggests that I need to put myself in settings where I'm likely to meet someone suitable. Yet I may take encouragement in knowing that if a relationship does develop, my availability will be a prime factor allowing God to arouse that person's interest in me. Simply being available is a step in the right direction if I want to find a partner.

Consider the example of Ruth. She had a lot going against her in her relationship with Boaz. She was a foreigner, a widow and not well off financially. Yet she was available for marriage, and she discreetly but clearly let him know (Ruth 3:1-13). The rest is history.

Making time for prayer. While much more could be said about the role of availability in using our gifts and seeking relationships, it's the area of prayer where I find this phenomenon most interesting. We easily become discouraged about the potential of our own prayers: *With so many Christians praying about so many matters, what difference will my prayers make?* Or, *I've prayed about this for two years—if God hasn't answered by now, I might as well give up.*

We tend to regard prayer much as we do the right to vote. While we consider it a great privilege, we doubt that our individual effort has much consequence. But while the voting analogy may accurately describe how we *feel* about prayer, it does not depict the actual potential of prayer at all. Scripture emphasizes that the effect of one person's prayer can be far-reaching.

This point impressed me forcefully some years ago while I was studying an unlikely portion of Scripture—1 Chronicles. I began my study of the book dutifully plodding through the seemingly endless genealogies which make up the first nine chapters, not expecting any deep inspiration or exceptional insights. I decided to read these chapters carefully, though. They are part of the history which the Holy Spirit has recorded, I reasoned, and I may miss some critical insight if I merely peruse them.

This scrutiny paid off, for in chapter 4 I encountered a remarkable statement which I had never noticed before. The writer notes that a woman gave birth to a son and named him Jabez, which sounds like the Hebrew word for pain, because his birth had been painful to her. This man "was more honorable than his brothers." One further detail is added about his life:

"Jabez cried out to the God of Israel, 'Oh, that you would bless me and enlarge my territory! Let your hand be with me, and keep me from harm so that I will be free from pain.' And God granted his request" (1 Chron 4:9-10). He whose name was Pain wanted God to protect him from a life of pain.

I was fascinated that the author thought it important to note that a man who is not mentioned elsewhere in Scripture prayed to God about a personal need. Why does he document this detail about Jabez's life, when he lists most of the other multitude of names in his genealogy without editorial comment?

The answer, I concluded, is that it is *unusual* for someone to petition God seriously about a need. It is *history* when one does so. Prayer itself is a *miracle* in the biblical understanding. The miracle is not that God answers the prayer—God is in the business of answering prayer. "And God granted his request." The miracle is that a person prays in the first place! Jabez was out of the ordinary.

When we have given serious attention to praying about a matter, we can trust that our prayer is effective *and* that our effort to pray is truly distinctive. We have done something few make the time to do earnestly. And we will receive benefits few position themselves to enjoy. While we cannot predict precisely how God will answer our prayer, we can be confident that things will be better because we have prayed and have opened ourselves more fully to his provision.

Here is a way in which each of us can have significant influence not only on the affairs of our own life but upon the movement of Christ in the world. As Andrew Murray expresses it:

> It is in very deed God's purpose that the fulfillment of His eternal purpose, and the coming of His kingdom, should depend on those of His people who, abiding in Christ, are ready to take up their position in Him their Head, the great Priest-King, and in their prayers are bold enough to say what they will that their God should do. As image-bearer and representative of God on earth, redeemed man has by his prayers to determine the history of this earth.[1]

Our availability for prayer makes the difference, not because there is power in prayer per se but because God has chosen to honor this effort. Let us take advantage of this unparalleled opportunity, which one writer has termed "life's limitless reach."

V

Rebounding from Disappointment and Failure

14

When Someone Lets You Down

Several months ago a woman in my Wednesday night class, Cary, asked a favor of me. The community where she lives has an unfortunate ordinance which could result in her losing the lease on her home. Cary has joined with other residents who may be affected to lobby for the policy's repeal. She asked if I would be willing to write a letter to the town council urging this change. I told her I'd be glad to help and promised to get the letter off quickly.

The following week I caught the flu, and then with the pressure of other responsibilities I never got around to fulfilling my promise. About six weeks later Cary brought up the matter again. Embarrassed, I confessed I had never followed through and began to offer my lame excuse, fearing she'd be disappointed with me. To my surprise she cut me off, saying, "Don't worry, the Lord withheld your hand." She went on to say that she realized now the timing wouldn't have been right for me to send the letter. She was glad I'd neglected to write it.

Not only was Cary's response gracious—and a great relief to

me—but it showed a remarkably broad-minded spirit. By saying "the Lord withheld your hand," she made it clear whose hand she believed was controlling this situation. And she was confident that God had used my foul-up not to her hurt but to her benefit.

I doubt a day goes by in your life or mine when someone doesn't disappoint us. A friend fails to call when she said she would. A neighbor forgets to return your rake. A colleague at work overlooks a lunch date with you. A promised delivery never arrives.

Or someone fails to live up to your expectations. Your child brings home a poor report card. A friend whose spiritual life you esteem drops out of Bible study. Your spouse doesn't affirm you as often as you'd like.

Or you experience rejection. A university turns down your application. A cherished job opportunity doesn't pan out. A relationship fizzles.

And there are times when we suffer actual injustice at the hands of others. Your boss blames you for a problem that wasn't your fault. A repair person charges you for work not done. Someone sideswipes your car and drives on.

When others let us down, it's normal not only to feel hurt but to think that our destiny has somehow been thwarted. We fear we've been cheated out of benefits which should rightfully be ours. It's the rare moment of faith when we consider that God may see things differently.

The Long View

More typically we feel God has pulled the rug out from under us. We're especially inclined to feel this way if we've prayed for a response from a certain person and it hasn't occurred. We feel cheated not only by that person but by God as well. We figure that if God were really on our side, he wouldn't have let this person disappoint us. After all, he ultimately has control over all human affairs, and he has promised to answer the prayers of his faithful.

But Scripture constantly emphasizes that God takes the long

view in looking after our welfare. This means that at times he will allow us to be disappointed in the short run for the sake of long-run benefits.

The Bible never promises that God will shield us from all possibility of being disappointed by others—even if we're walking fully in his will. Nor does it suggest that God should be expected to override someone else's free will and cause a quick change in the way that person treats us, simply because we've prayed. Genuine change in behavior takes time. And God follows his own timetable in changing a person's heart. The brothers of Joseph, in the Genesis story, are a case in point. So is the Egyptian Pharaoh whom Moses petitioned on behalf of the Israelites.

Consider, too, that while Jesus consistently granted requests for personal healing during his earthly ministry, he generally refused petitions to make a sudden change in one person's conduct toward another. He denied a man's request that he persuade the man's brother to share his inheritance, for instance (Lk 2:13-14), and Martha's plea that he exhort Mary to help her (Lk 10:38-42).

God will not necessarily bring an immediate change in someone's behavior toward us in response to our prayer. We should, by all means, continue to raise such requests boldly to God and trust that he will answer them as he sees best. Yet we can take comfort in knowing that if people don't treat us as we've prayed they would, it doesn't mean God has turned his back on us. It's more likely that our expectations have been unrealistic.

We can take even greater comfort in the clear and unequivocal teaching of Scripture that God uses all of the actions of others toward us—whether for good or ill—to further his best intentions for us.

A Surprising Response

It's here that the example of Joseph is so instructive. No one in Scripture had better reason for being resentful toward family members than he did. His brothers hated him so greatly that they sold him to slave traders, who carried him to Egypt and sold him there. Through a unique series of events, including several years in prison, Joseph became second-in-command to Pharaoh and director of a masterful famine relief effort. A severe food shortage ravaged the Mideast, and Joseph's brothers traveled to Egypt seeking grain. Some twenty years after selling him into bondage they stood before him humbly seeking his help, having no inkling he was their flesh and blood.

At this point Joseph had one of the most exceptional opportunities for revenge one could imagine. Yet he found it within himself not only to forgive his brothers radically from the heart—well before they asked him to—but to encourage them to move their families en masse to Egypt. There he provided lavishly for them for the remainder of their lives.

Joseph's astonishing capacity to forgive his iron-hearted kin sprang from an unusually deep trust that God was controlling his life—using even calamities to bring about his good purpose. At the moment when revenge could have been the sweetest, he swept away all basis by declaring to his brothers, "Do not be distressed and do not be angry with yourselves for selling me here, because it was to save lives that God sent me ahead of you to preserve for you a remnant on earth and to save your lives by a great deliverance. So then, it was not you who sent me here, but God" (Gen 45:5-8).

Some years later when their father Jacob died, his brothers feared that Joseph might cave in to repressed revenge. But with additional years of hindsight he insisted even more emphatically, "Don't be afraid. Am I in the place of God? You intended to harm me, but God intended it for good to accomplish what is now being done, the saving of many lives. So then, don't be afraid. I will provide for you and your children" (Gen 50:19-21).

What makes Joseph's attitude so enviable is that its redemptive impact was so pervasive. The benefit to Joseph alone was substantial. We don't sense that he was being eaten up with bitterness during his years in exile. Resentment would have consumed much of his creative energy. Yet he displayed social and practical skills that won the respect of the jailkeeper, the king's servants and ultimately Pharaoh himself. This suggests that he managed to stay optimistic during much of this time.

Then there was the extensive benefit to the people of Egypt and the surrounding world—the saving of thousands of lives. Finally, there were extraordinary benefits to his own family: Joseph and his brothers were reconciled; his brothers matured remarkably; numerous members of his extended family were saved from starvation.

The Promise and the Challenge

The message, then, is one of indescribable encouragement for us who follow Christ. Here in the beginning of Scripture we're shown that God uses even the most adverse actions of others to our benefit and to bring about his best purposes for us. It is foundational to faith in Christ to embrace this belief in the wholehearted way in which Joseph did.

When others disappoint us, we can trust there are hidden benefits. In time, with the marvelous advantage of hindsight, these will become evident. Such confidence in God's providence will lead not only to deeper personal joy but to greater effectiveness in our work for Christ. And the impact of our attitude will be felt by many.

Yet we come back to the fact that this sort of outlook is difficult to achieve. It is not a natural way of thinking but a challenging perspective of faith. How, then, do we do it? The most helpful step we can take is to confront our frustrations during our daily devotional time. Spending time in quiet, prayerful reflection about our struggles and disappointments with other people can make all the difference. If someone has disappointed us, we should strive to think of ways God may use that letdown to our benefit. We should remind ourselves that God has the best in mind for us and that what we view as a setback may be seen quite differently by him. It's important, too, to pray for patience and the fullest measure of wisdom God is willing to give us.

It also helps to try to understand the motives of those who disappoint us. It may be that their behavior had nothing to do with disliking us but resulted from personal weakness or extenuating circumstances. Even if they really did want to hurt us, this doesn't mean they will always feel this way toward us. God may change their hearts, as he did with Joseph's brothers. Our ability to forgive them and believe the best for them can help that to happen.

This isn't to say that we should never express disappointment or anger to someone else. There are times when confronting someone is necessary not only for our own emotional health but for their growth as well. Love must be tough at times. God never expects us to be a doormat to anyone. We need to learn to be appropriately assertive, to own our feelings, to stand firm for what God has called us to do even when others are not supportive. This is all very important.

First Things First
Yet our greatest need—far and away—is to appreciate God's creative sovereignty in our life and his infinite concern for us. When that perspective is right, our negative feelings toward others often dissolve. Genuine forgiveness becomes possible. And when confronting someone is necessary, we are able to do it in a more relaxed, confident spirit.

The bottom line is that God is not our adversary but our friend. We can't remind ourselves of this too often. If the example of Joseph isn't convincing enough, he has given us his clear promise in Romans 8:28: "We know that in all things God works for the good of those who love him, who have been called according to his purpose." And to make the point even more emphatically, Paul reiterates it in different words three verses later: "if God is for us, who can be against us?" (Rom 8:31).

The friendship of Christ is the overriding factor that touches every relationship and encounter of life. In this matter he has not withheld his hand.

15

The Problem of Unanswered Prayer

It really seemed that filling the concert hall would be a cinch. The Sons of Thunder had rented a 4,000-seat civic center in Salisbury, Maryland, and scheduled a concert which we hoped would attract hordes of Christians from around Maryland's Eastern Shore. To be sure, we had never staged a concert outside the Washington, D.C., area, and Salisbury was several hours away.

But we understood the effect of good publicity. We got an attractive poster printed, mailed it to all the churches in the region and tacked it up in every conceivable public spot.

More important, we understood the effect of fervent prayer. Another member of the band and I agreed to claim the promise of Matthew 18:19 that if two believers are united in praying for anything, it will be accomplished for them. We committed ourselves to pray frequently and earnestly that God would fill the auditorium to capacity. And we prayed with considerable confidence that our request would be granted.

But on the evening of the concert you could have shot a cannon through the auditorium and not hit anyone. The 350 people who did show up were enthusiastic and a respectable audience by many standards. But to me the vast number of empty seats meant not only financial disaster but spiritual defeat. I had poured my heart into prayers which didn't reap even a ten-percent response!

My experience wasn't unique. Most of us have gone through discouraging and perhaps puzzling episodes of unanswered prayer. A relationship that we begged God for didn't work out. A job interview which we diligently prayed about fizzled. A financial investment bathed in prayer turned sour. A request for healing wasn't granted.

The problem wouldn't be so vexing if the biblical promises about prayer weren't so numerous and explicit. But time and again Scripture declares that specific prayer brings specific results. "I chose you . . . that whatever you ask the Father in my name, he may give it to you" (Jn 15:16 RSV). This verse and many others say that God specializes in giving us what we ask! Yet, unless we are very unusual, we don't live the Christian life very long without some serious bubble-popping in this area. What we say is not always what we get.

Typically we begin the Christian life very optimistic about the possibilities of prayer; then we have some disappointing experiences with prayer and skepticism sets in. Few experiences pose a greater challenge to our faith.

Explaining the Puzzle

We grope for an explanation to our experiences of unanswered prayer. Many times we attribute the problem to lack of faith. We just didn't believe strongly enough. Indeed, this can be the problem. Yet there are many examples in Scripture of anxious, ambivalent people receiving what they ask from God.

Other times we ring it up to bad motives. We weren't really praying "in Jesus' name." Again, motives can be the culprit, as James

4:3 reminds us. To pray in Jesus' name means to pray with a desire for his will and glory. Yet we can so "mystify" the idea of praying in Jesus' name that we cease to believe that God is interested in what *we* think. As Andrew Murray notes, the thrust of the biblical promises is that God limits much of what he does on earth to what his people are bold enough to request through prayer.

But more often than not there is another explanation which is far less appreciated. We underestimate the difficulty of really *wanting* God to do what we're asking. The sort of agreement Matthew 18:19 encourages is an extremely difficult mental state to experience. For one thing, as modern psychology has shown, we are largely subconscious creatures. We may seem to desire something on the surface yet underneath greatly resist it.

In addition, we don't know our future; only God does. He knows that what we will desire in five years may be strikingly different from what we passionately crave right now. Would granting our present petition really be giving us what we desire in terms of a lifetime?

I now believe that if God had fulfilled my request for a packed concert hall, a deeper, more important desire for spiritual growth and wisdom would have been denied. I would have been left thinking that Christian programs can be carried out without the intensive personal contact work so necessary for effective ministry. Further, I might have become more locked into a music career and been less free to consider teaching, which in time I discovered was more in line with the gifts God has given me. I can now say wholeheartedly that God did me a great favor in allowing me to experience disappointment that evening.

I believe that most of the experiences of unanswered prayer which we have as followers of Christ can be explained in this way. It's not that God has refused to grant us our desires—he has simply understood them better than we have. Appreciating this can do wonders to keep us from losing heart when our prayers seem to go unheeded.

Staying Hopeful

Understanding this will help us find the incentive to keep praying, for it is through continuing prayer that our desires become clarified. Some grow stronger. Others fade away and we're grateful that God refrained from granting them!

I'm not suggesting, then, that we shouldn't be bold and specific in raising our desires to God. Quite the contrary: Scripture commands us in many places to do exactly that. Jesus' parable of the importunate widow (Lk 18:1-8) is a dramatic reminder that there are times when long-term persistence in prayer is not only permitted but expected. Jesus told the parable that we might "always pray and not lose heart" (Lk 18:1). Clearly he meant that we shouldn't give up praying about *specific personal concerns,* no matter how long it takes to receive an answer.

Indeed, we will probably be surprised at how frequently the answer that comes does correspond closely with the prayer we have made. I'm convinced that if anyone gives serious attention to prayer over a sufficient period of time, and broadens her horizons to pray about a number of concerns, she will have enough positive experiences to convince her that God is truly interested in answering her prayers. If we hang in there, we'll discover that God is more abundantly willing to grant our petitions than we've imagined.

I can happily say that as I've continued to walk with Christ, there have been enough affirming experiences with prayer to convince me that this is true. My confidence that God answers prayer springs not only from biblical teaching but from personal experience as well. But it has taken time for that conviction to grow into a strong and abiding one. I suspect that this will be the case with most of us.

We may experience some disappointment in the short run. But as we continue to give prayer the attention it deserves, we'll find over time that our investment is greatly rewarded.

16

Winning Through Failure

Christian *psychiatrist Paul Tournier writes about one of his* most humiliating experiences, which occurred when he spoke at a university assembly. "I felt right from the first word that I was not going to make contact with my audience. I clung to my notes and laboriously recited with growing nervousness, what I had to say. As the audience left I could see my friends slipping hurriedly away. . . . On the way home in my car with my wife, I burst into tears."[1]

The next day a professor of philosophy phoned him and said that Tournier's talk was indeed the worst he had ever heard. But he added that he had sat through innumerable erudite lectures in his lifetime which left no impression on him, yet somehow he was drawn to Tournier. A lasting friendship between the two developed, which resulted in the professor's becoming a Christian. Tournier writes of looking back upon the disastrous lecture as one of the great successes of his life.

His experience reminds us that God so often sees success and failure in different terms than we do. One of the most unfortunate effects of failure is the pessimistic outlook it brings on. We start imagining all sorts of dreadful consequences coming from our bungled effort. Ironically, our failure may be a success in God's mind, contributing in a most positive way to our future and to his intentions for our life.

I think of several disappointments in dating which I had when I was single, where relationships did not develop as I wished. In each case my sense of failure was so overwhelming that I saw my future cast in concrete as a miserable, lonely person. Today I look on those experiences quite differently. Not only did I learn volumes, but the no's—so painful to hear at the time—eventually cleared the way for a yes from one who was much better suited to be my life mate.

Losing the Battle

There are, to be sure, times when failure is more than just a perceived experience. There are times when we have clearly fallen short not only of our own standards but of God's. Here it becomes especially difficult to feel positive about failure.

A military defeat of the Israelites in Joshua 7 is instructive. The Jews have experienced many successes in battle under Joshua and have become headstrong. Now they decide to take on Ai with only a few thousand soldiers, greatly underestimating their opponent's strength. In addition, they don't know that one of their number, Achan, has taken some "devoted" items from a previous battle—items which God commanded destroyed—thus arousing God's wrath against Israel.

Ai chases back Israel's army and kills thirty-six men. Though it is a relatively minor defeat, "the hearts of the [Israelites] melted and became like water" (v. 5). Joshua, devastated, wallows on the ground and prays, "Ah, Sovereign LORD, why did you ever bring this people across the Jordan to deliver us into the hands of the Amorites to destroy us? . . . The Canaanites and the other people of the country will hear about this and will surround us and wipe out our name from the earth" (vv 6-9).

God does not debate Joshua's predictions of doom but gives him practical instruction: he is to rid Israel of the one who has taken the devoted things. Joshua obeys. Then God tells him to take *all* the fighting men and attack Ai again. This time Israel has a resounding victory.

The Israelites gained two immeasurable benefits from their defeat with Ai: a deeper awareness of where they were vulnerable to sinning against God, and a sharper understanding of the logistics necessary to rout a formidable foe. When they repented and put their new insights into action, they became remarkably successful at a point of previous failure.

Winning the War

When we know we have displeased God, we're often tempted to remain at the wallowing stage. Like Joshua, we cannot see past our failure, and all our thoughts are colored by it. "God intends to keep punishing me, and the whole future is on a roll against me," we suppose. At such times we must put into practice everything we know about repentance and the grace and forgiveness of Christ.

But we must also take into account everything we know about the creative power of God. He is speaking to us as he did to Joshua, telling us to learn what we can from our failure and to move on. Through failure we can gain vital insights into ourselves—our strengths and limitations—which may not come any other way.

And, as Tournier's experience reminds us, failure may have more than just educational value. The failure may in fact be a success which we don't yet recognize. There are times when we don't live up to our own expectations but fulfill God's quite well.

All of this is not to suggest that we are ever to court failure. As Christians we're called to excellence and diligence in what we do. But too often the fear of failure keeps us from taking the risks necessary to build relationships and develop our potential for Christ.

In their popular book *In Search of Excellence,* Thomas Peters and Robert Waterman note that the most productive American corporations encourage their employees to be comfortable with failing. A certain number of failures are necessary to produce an effective product or to make a breakthrough in research. Without the freedom to fail, creativity is stifled.[2] So, in the workplace and in our daily lives, failing can be a necessary and good thing—a means to growth and eventual success.

And how much more is this true with our service for Christ! There are few principles of the Christian life more important to learn. We must not fail at this point.

17

It's Okay Not to Feel OK

A young man recently told me of the misfortunes which have befallen his mother. During the past year her husband divorced her after less than five years of marriage. It was a painful separation for this sixty-five-year-old woman, whose first husband died when she was sixty. Now she has been diagnosed with a terminal illness. And her family has decided, against her will, to commit her to a nursing home.

He then added, almost as an afterthought, "She's also suffering from depression."

I thought, *My soul! Who wouldn't be depressed under such circumstances!*

This man's remark reflects a way of thinking about depression which has become commonplace during the twentieth century. Rather than say that someone *feels* depressed, we say that they are "suffering from depression." Such language suggests that depression is an illness—that you "have" depression just as you would have the flu or tuberculosis. An elaborate vocabulary has evolved for describing varieties and levels of depression.

Many use such terminology about depression innocently and with the best intentions. Yet it reveals that modern society feels uneasy with depression. We think of it as an abnormal, unhealthy condition.

The effect of this attitude on depressed persons is often devastating. They wonder if their despondent feelings mean that they are emotionally ill. They become depressed that they're depressed, and their condition is aggravated considerably.

Concern with relieving the distress about depression which troubles so many has led psychologist Lesley Hazelton to write a gracious and redemptive book, *The Right to Feel Bad: Coming to Terms with Normal Depression.* Most depression, Hazelton argues, is not mental illness or breakdown but a normal process of dealing with loss. In time it always passes. She chastises both society and the psychological profession for being too quick to categorize depression as an inappropriate response to life's challenges. She states bluntly, "Calling someone 'a depressive' is a means of labeling that person. . . . The world needs the label, not the depressed person."[1]

Beyond the Stiff Upper Lip

Hazelton also insists that depression is often beneficial to us. Through it we grow and deepen in ways which cannot come through any other process. Though she does not write from an explicitly Christian perspective, I find Scripture in strong support of her claims. There is simply no basis in the Bible for the popular assumption that the Christian should be continually euphoric.

Scripture recognizes sorrow as basic to compassion, for instance. The ability to feel remorse over the misfortunes of others is one of the key qualities of empathy (Jn 11:35, 38). Feeling the hurt that others feel is needed if I am to have godly indignation toward injustice. If I can't identify emotionally with another's pain, I'll not be able to love that person in a genuinely Christian way.

But even when it comes to our own personal losses and setbacks, Scripture shows that grief can be a normal and beneficial response. Consider how often people in the Bible spent days lamenting the death of loved ones (Gen 23:2; 37:34; 50:3, 10; Num 20:29; Deut 34:8; Acts 8:2). A clearing of the mind comes through mourning a personal defeat. It's often a necessary part of coming to terms with the loss and putting it behind us.

Christian writer Walter Trobisch notes:

There is a courage involved in being depressed. There is such a thing as the gift of depression—a gift which enables us to be "heavy" to live with what is difficult. Once I heard an experienced psychiatrist say, "All people of worth and value have depressions." Indeed, shallow, superficial people seldom have depressions. It requires a certain inner substance and depth of mind to be depressed.[2]

We ought, then, not to think of depression as something people "suffer from." We should see it, rather, as a normal response to disappointment. It's part of the process of working through a personal setback and coming to the point of positively accepting God's will. And the ability to feel depressed is needed if we are to share effectively in the sorrow and sufferings of others.

Grief and Optimism

This isn't to say that the Christian outlook shouldn't be substantially optimistic. Indeed it should! Paul admonishes us, "whatever is true, whatever is noble, whatever is right, whatever is pure, whatever is lovely, whatever is admirable—if anything is excellent or praiseworthy—think about such things" (Phil 4:8). We should strive to develop as optimistic an attitude as possible. We should dwell on the positive, making a conscious effort to remember the blessings of God that have meant the most to us. We should thank him constantly for his mercy, his forgiveness, his empowering grace and the distinctive gifts and opportunities he has given us. We should do whatever we reasonably can to overcome depression—through counseling, prayer, positive "self-talk" and keeping a good measure of momentum in our life.

Yet we shouldn't think it incompatible with an optimistic attitude toward life to have periods of sorrow and discouragement.
Such times may be necessary for our own adjustment to loss or for
stretching our heart to empathize with the misfortunes of others. In
spite of his supremely vibrant spirit, Paul talked freely of a time of
personal loss when his sufferings were so great that he "despaired
of life itself" (2 Cor 1:8 RSV). And the empathy he felt toward his
fellow Jews was so intense that he experienced "great sorrow and
unceasing anguish" over their fate for rejecting Christ (Rom 9:1-2).

Indeed, to regard depression as an acceptable condition is itself
an optimistic outlook. This perspective will allow us to stay hopeful during times of grief. And it will enable us to better handle our
depression: to work through it, accept the loss that triggered it and
move on. It's the belief that depression is an aberration from healthy
emotional life that makes us vulnerable to prolonged and debilitating periods of being down.

We should resist the temptation to label depression as illness or
neurosis. While there are instances where it signifies a serious condition, most depression is an understandable response to disappointment. Others who are depressed need our compassion, not our labels.
We should be equally careful not to stigmatize ourselves when we
feel depressed. God has built into each of us a wonderfully com-
plex emotional fabric. He has given us the capacity to experience a
wide variety of emotions. Indeed, much of the key to enjoying the
highs is learning to accept the lows. Depression can be a gift of
God, to help us emotionally let go of the past so that we can embrace his will for our future more wholeheartedly.

18

Fresh Starts

It wasn't my first romantic disappointment by any means. I had been through several difficult experiences in junior high and high school. But now in college, with all the optimism of being a new Christian, I simply wasn't prepared for it. I had set my heart on winning the affection of a certain woman in our college fellowship. Finally we talked and I shared my dreams of a serious relationship with her. When she told me firmly that we could never be more than friends, I was devastated.

I was in such a state of shock that I knew I needed help. The next morning I phoned the youth pastor at our church, who agreed to meet with me that afternoon. While I knew I needed his counsel, I dreaded talking with him. I feared he would give me a lecture on renunciation or something.

But far from putting a spiritual Band-Aid on my hurt, he gave me some eminently practical advice. He expressed his counsel in a metaphor which spoke perfectly to my situation: "If you have a glass filled with dirty water, there are two ways to remove the water from the glass. You can dump it out, which gets rid of the water but leaves the glass empty. Or you can take a pitcher of clear, clean water and begin pouring it into the glass. Gradually the fresh water displaces the dirty water."

The empty glass, he explained, could represent the unhealthy response to rejection. You pull out of life and shield yourself from people. You may dwell on your hurt feelings or repress them. But you stay isolated, safe from being rejected again. Still, you remain emotionally drained, since nothing is filling the void left by the broken relationship.

Pouring fresh water into the glass, on the other hand, represents the route to emotional healing. Far from ignoring your feelings of disappointment, you face them and acknowledge them. At the same time you stay socially active and take steps to build new relationships. Gradually the new life which comes from these fresh experiences replaces the anguish that now seems so overpowering.

Substantial Healing

Within a week I found the courage to ask out another woman in the fellowship, and the experience was rejuvenating to me. My hurt feelings continued to gnaw at me for some time. But new friendships, and eventually marriage itself, brought substantial healing. Even today it is not impossible to jog myself back into the feelings of that hoped-for relationship of many years ago. But I can also say with gratitude that I'm glad now that it didn't work out.

Disappointments in relationships are inevitable in life. Being a Christian in no way insulates us from them. These disappointments aren't limited to romance, but include broken friendships, all the varieties of family strife and separation which are so wrenching, and the indescribable void brought on by the death of a friend or loved one.

God never expects us to react to such disappointments like spiritual robots. The most godly people in Scripture showed a considerable capacity for experiencing sorrow and grief. Jesus himself wept over the death of his friend Lazarus and showed anguish over the beheading of John the Baptist.

At the same time, we must not allow ourselves to lose sight of the renewing grace of God. The book of Ruth gives us one of Scripture's most inspiring pictures of individuals making a fresh start in relationships. Naomi, bereft of her husband and both sons, assumes life has little left to offer her. "Do not call me Naomi, call me Mara [bitter]," she declares to her townspeople upon returning to Bethlehem from Moab. "I went away full, and the LORD has brought me back empty" (Ruth 1:20-21 RSV).

But Ruth, her daughter-in-law, remarries and has a son, and the relationship with this grandchild fills a gaping emotional need in Naomi's life. Naomi's friends announce to her, "Blessed be the LORD, who has not left you this day without next of kin; and may his name be renowned in Israel! He shall be to you a restorer of life and a nourisher of your old age; for your daughter-in-law who loves you, who is more to you than seven sons, has borne him" (Ruth 4:14-15 RSV). Ruth bears a child whom the townspeople declare will be a restorer of life to his grandmother Naomi in her old age. Yet the child was *God's* gift, and the passage shows that God himself was a restorer of life to Ruth, at an unlikely point in her life. We scarcely find a more encouraging and stirring aspect of God's nature revealed anywhere in Scripture. We are reminded that it is central to his nature to bring emotional healing and renewal even to our social life, and even at points when we assume all hope is lost. Appreciating this way in which God restores our lives inspires us to take steps that will allow it to happen.

Redirection of Affection

We should dwell on this aspect of God's nature—that he is a restorer of life—when we experience the pain of rejection or a failed relationship. God may choose to bring healing by restoring the relationship itself. If not, he can be trusted to redirect our feelings and open up new opportunities. Disappointment, in fact, can bring depth

and empathy to our lives which will enhance the quality of relationships in the future.

God is even capable of giving you romantic love for a new individual. As horridly academic as that may sound if you're reeling
from a broken relationship, I can simply assure you from my own
experience—and that of many others—that it's true. In the book of
Ruth, it is not only Naomi who experiences emotional healing, but
also Ruth, who remarries. Boaz was Ruth's *second* husband; once
again, she finds the capacity for romantic love toward someone.

If we are to personally experience God's healing, though, we
must take those steps which allow him to pour fresh water into the
glass. That's why participating in Christian fellowship and seeking
out new friendships is so important. Staying in circulation is critical.

Naomi and Ruth didn't enjoy the full benefits of God's renewal
until they left Moab, the place of their bereavement, and moved to
Judah. It must have been very difficult for them to leave the old
familiar territory. Yet this move made possible the wonderful new
family relationships which developed for both of them. Of course,
Naomi didn't bottle up her feelings when she made this move. Far
from it! She bore her grief fully and expressed it freely. Undoubtedly Ruth did too. Yet even in the midst of their sorrow they found
the courage to take an important step of faith toward healing. It is a
graphic example of pouring fresh water into the glass.

May God grant us such courage to move forward when we
personally experience disappointment. And may he give us the wisdom to understand the steps we can take which will most fully open
us to his healing. May we never lose sight of God's role as a restorer of life or doubt his ability to meet our deepest needs. And
may we never forget the benefits of making a fresh start when a
relationship has ended and our world seems to be coming apart.

VI

Gaining Focus for Steps of Faith

19

My Desires
and God's Will

Malcolm *hated his job as much as anyone I've known.* Though many would find the profession of house painting enjoyable, to him it was merely a means of paying the rent. He sat slumped in the chair across from my desk, bemoaning his lot.

Yet Malcolm was a Christian who wanted God's will. So I stopped him and asked, "If God rolled out the red carpet and said you could be in any career you wished, which would it be?"

He didn't have to think long. He shot back, "I'd like to be an English teacher."

Malcolm had two years of college behind him. I was confident he could go back, finish and find a job in the public school system. So I said, "You're young enough to do it. Why don't you pursue teaching with all the passion and energy you can muster?"

His reply was unforgettable. "I know that God doesn't want me teaching. I'd enjoy the experience too much. And the affirmation of students would be more than I could handle." Then he added the clincher: He was certain God wanted him painting houses, for he thoroughly disliked his work!

An extreme example, unquestionably. Yet it reflects a pattern of thinking that I've often observed in Christians and sometimes have fallen into myself. It's the notion that being in God's will means by definition choosing to do something unpleasant. God wouldn't possibly want you in a career that you find enjoyable, it's assumed, for unhealthy aspirations would surely get in the way.

Actually, I know of an example even more extreme than Malcolm's. A student about to graduate from Princeton Seminary decided to enroll in medical school. When an astonished professor asked him why he made this atypical choice, he replied that after considering all the alternatives, he found medical work the least appealing. He concluded, then, that this must be the profession that God wanted him to enter.

Instincts Good and Bad

It's not hard to understand how Malcolm and the seminary graduate reached their conclusions about God's will. Scripture has plenty to say about the dangers of trusting our gut instincts. "The heart is deceitful above all things and beyond cure," Jeremiah declares (Jer 17:9).

Perhaps the most notorious biblical example of the heart's deceit is David's attraction to Bathsheba. David was so devoted to the Lord that he is held up throughout Scripture as the ideal of a godly person. Yet he committed not only adultery but murder because of his enchantment with this woman. I suspect that David may well have rationalized his actions as being in God's will. Since his feelings for Bathsheba were so strong, he may have thought that God was prompting him through them to do something which he never would have considered in a less-crazed moment. "It can't be wrong, when it feels so right."

There was another occasion when David followed his natural impulses and got into trouble. He took a census of Israel. David's action was so repugnant to God that he punished the entire nation with a ravaging plague (1 Chron 21).

We might conclude from such examples that we're always on shaky ground to follow the instincts of the heart. Yet David demonstrates another and very important side to the story. His call from God to be king of Israel placed him in a role that he thoroughly enjoyed. He found military life stimulating, he thrived on making administrative decisions, and he cherished the opportunity to be a spiritual leader of the people. David did not in any way think of his position as—to use the modern and not quite biblical term—"a sacrificial vocation." While there were plenty of sacrifices to be made *within* the position, he relished the role itself.

I'm certain that David's remarkable effectiveness as king was due in large part to the fact that he enjoyed his work so much. Because the job reflected his temperament so well, he was able to pour his full creative energies into it. Saul, his predecessor, had considerably less aspiration to be king (1 Sam 9:21; 10:21-22). His performance in that role was also much less impressive.

Fulfillment and Fruitfulness
Think back over your life for a moment. Who have been the teachers who had the greatest impact on you? How about the pastors or spiritual leaders? I'm willing to guess it has been the ones who found the greatest enjoyment in their work.

This has certainly been true in my own life. I had little interest in academics during junior high and high school. While my lackluster performance in school was largely my own fault, it also seemed that many of my teachers were not highly motivated. Two of them, though—a French instructor and a public-speaking teacher—did succeed in penetrating my boredom, because their excitement for their subjects was contagious. I worked hard for them.

It has been the same in the spiritual area. I attended several different churches growing up but was never greatly influenced by any of their pastors or teachers. Many of them seemed possessed with a grim sense of duty and showed little zest for life. I wanted no part of such dreariness. When I began attending Fourth Presbyterian Church in college, the atmosphere was strikingly different. Those on the pastoral staff were exuberant and took obvious pleasure in their work. Their enthusiasm was stimulating, and my spiritual life grew by leaps and bounds.

Those who have been the greatest help to me have almost always been ones who enjoyed their work. This has been true in every area. Including house painting. Not long after talking with Malcolm I hired him to paint my garage. His work was slow and mediocre. Though he was capable of doing a much better job, he simply wasn't motivated.

It's inescapable. We do our best work for Christ when it's a reflection of what we most want to do.

Energized

While Scripture has plenty to say about the evils of the desires of the flesh, it also brings out another and deeply encouraging aspect of human desire that has received far too little emphasis in Christian teaching. It proclaims that God himself creates certain desires within us who follow Christ in order to guide us in certain directions.

In Psalm 139 David talks specifically about God's guidance in his life and how it relates to his own aspirations. He declares, "For you created my inmost being" (v. 13). The term "inmost being"—literally, "kidneys"—was the most significant word the Hebrews had for indicating the personality. David is saying that God has given him a unique temperament. This meant that God had put within him the inclination to enjoy certain work and roles. In speaking about himself, David conveyed a truth which applies to all people.

Paul makes a similar point specifically about Christians in Philippians 2:12-13, though our English translations often miss the full impact of his language. "Work out your own salvation with fear and trembling; for God is at work in you, both to will and to work for his good pleasure" (RSV). Paul urges us here to make responsible decisions. The phrase "work out your own salvation" doesn't mean *achieve* your salvation, for Paul is writing to those who are already saved. He is telling us, rather, to work out the *implications* of the salvation which we already possess. We should make careful decisions in accord with God's will.

We are *able* to do this, Paul goes on to explain, because God is working within us to see that we carry out his will. Twice in the passage he uses the verb *work,* which in the Greek is *energeo*—the root of our word *energy.* Paul is literally saying, then, "God is *energizing* you." God is giving us motivation to do what he wants us to do!

Scripture pictures this process of energizing as one of the chief functions of the Holy Spirit. Jesus implied this when he termed the Holy Spirit a "Counselor" (Jn 14:16). The Greek term meant a military official responsible for giving fresh courage and inspiration to soldiers who had lost heart in the heat of battle.

Interestingly, the most common role of the Holy Spirit in the Old Testament is that of a motivator. Pick up a concordance and look up references to the Spirit in the Old Testament, and you'll see what I mean. When the Holy Spirit comes upon individuals, he gives them passion and fire to do what God is calling them to do— a far cry from the placid understanding of the Holy Spirit emphasized in much teaching today and in so many of our hymns.

We should expect, then, that if God is leading us to make a major commitment of our lives, he'll give us some passion for what we're undertaking. We'll be motivated for the task. There's something neurotically misplaced about the notion that we ought to follow the alternative we least desire.

Healthy Self-Denial

But how does this possibly reconcile with the frequent biblical admonitions to *deny* our desires? Part of the answer lies in the quality of our walk with Christ. If I'm taking my relationship with Christ seriously and making an effort to grow spiritually, I can be confident that many of my desires are being inspired by him. I can trust, too, that many desires which I would otherwise experience are not coming to the surface.

This is only part of the answer, however. There is also a rule of thumb which is extremely important to understand. To best explain this, it helps to use the term *vocation* in its original Reformation sense. Luther and Calvin used *vocation* to mean not only one's profession but any major commitment or status in a person's life. In their understanding, not only is my job a vocation, but also my family relationships, my involvement with my church, and any other significant investment of my time and energy.

With this in mind, here is a principle which should govern most of our major decisions as Christians: *A decision for a vocation should be based as much as possible upon our personal desires.* We ought to read them as a vital sign of how God has made us and wants us to direct our energies for Christ. *But in the day-to-day decisions made within vocations, we should deny ourselves in every way necessary to be an effective servant to others and to faithfully fulfill our responsibilities.* In this case, then, self-denial takes place *within* our areas of motivation rather than outside of them.

When Paul speaks about the vocation of marriage, for instance, he stresses that much personal sacrifice and discipline are needed to be an effective spouse and parent (Eph 5:21—6:4). Yet he also insists that you should marry only if your desire for marriage is strong (1 Cor 7). So self-denial occurs within an area of life where you truly want to be.

Or consider Paul's teaching on the qualifications for a spiritual leader. In 1 Timothy 3 he notes many marks of self-denial and discipline needed by an effective "bishop," or spiritual shepherd. Yet often overlooked is the fact that he begins his instructions saying, "If any one aspires to the office of bishop, he desires a noble task" (v. 1 RSV). Paul simply assumes that the good spiritual leader will be strongly motivated for the role. Self-denial takes place within that overriding desire.

This same principle applies to other vocations we enter as Christians, to the extent that God allows us freedom of choice. We should follow our desires in choosing them, then deny our desires as necessary to faithfully carry them out.

This isn't to overlook the challenge often involved in determining what our most significant desires are. Considerable prayer, counsel and experimenting may be needed to understand them. Yet as we come to recognize which desires are deepest and most consistent within us, we gain a treasured window into how God has fashioned our life. As he allows us freedom of choice, we should make vocational choices which respect this insight.

God has made your life to be a gift to others. And a cheerful giver gives the best gift!

20

You're a Gift
to Others—
But Not a Savior

During *my senior year of college I worked with a youth minis-*try team at Fourth Presbyterian Church. We were a bunch of over-achievers and, given the multitude of youth and programs in this active metropolitan church, that meant certain fatigue for many of us.

At a staff meeting one Sunday afternoon a member complained to the youth pastor that many of us were feeling considerably over-taxed. He responded that we must learn to place some limits on ourselves.

"But," she replied, "Jesus never turned his back on any person's need."

As quickly as the words left her lips he shot back, *"But you're not Jesus Christ!"*

At that moment it was as though giant chains dropped from my body. As a young Christian I simply assumed I was to imitate Jesus in every way possible. This meant striving to live at his energy level and following his pattern of continually responding to an over-whelming variety of needs.

For the first time it dawned on me that there was a difference between how Jesus ministered to people and how I was expected to do so. God had put me within a certain physical shell, and I was to operate within its limitations. Not only was it okay to pace my-self—I was *required* to do so. What a glorious insight!

Many Christians never make this liberating discovery. I've known many who feel such an obligation to attend to every need which comes their way that they are constantly exhausted. They become saturated with responsibility within their church, work or community.

This same attitude leads some to sink into demeaning relation-ships, where they feel obliged to do whatever is necessary to keep the other person happy. Marsha, a single woman in her thirties, put it this way: "Many times I've ended up in unsatisfying relation-ships with men and not had the courage to break away. I feel com-pelled to be a *savior* to them. I can't manage the thought of hurting them. I do what I think will please them, even if it means sacrific-ing my own interests or becoming less of a person myself."

Appreciate Your Distinctiveness
Marsha's words—"I feel compelled to be a savior"—well describe how we felt on the youth ministry team. We were trying to *be* Christ to others rather than simply letting him use us as his instruments. Little wonder we were burning out in the process.

As I've grown in my understanding of what it means to serve Christ, I've found it helpful to think of my role as being a gift to other people, rather than a savior—which Christ alone can be to them. Paul suggests this perspective in Ephesians 4, when he refers to people in certain callings as gifts. "And his gifts were that some should be apostles, some prophets, some evangelists, some pastors and teachers" (v. 11 RSV). While Paul speaks elsewhere of God *giving* gifts to people, he speaks here of individuals *being* gifts. As the NIV expresses it, "It was he who gave some" to fulfill different callings (Eph 4:11). I'm certain that he meant the thought of individuals being a gift to apply not only to those in the roles mentioned but to all Christians (v. 7). Each of us who follows Christ is a unique gift from him to the body of Christ and the world.

I like the notion of being a gift, for while it suggests that we have considerable responsibility to others, it puts our obligation in right perspective.

For one thing, being a gift means that the burden ultimately rests with God, who gives to others through us. There is great rest in knowing that *he* is doing the giving. Our responsibility is simply to learn to respond to him, so that he will be able to make us the gift he intended. It's to this end that Jesus promised, "My yoke is easy and my burden is light" (Mt 11:30).

Being a gift also brings to mind our distinctiveness. A gift is special because it is distinctive. Scripture constantly attests to the fact that God fashions each of our lives differently, in order to make us each a unique gift to others. Throughout the pages of Scripture we encounter hundreds of individuals who were loyal to God and did his will yet displayed profound individuality. Never do we sense that God wanted any of his servants to become a clone of any other.

God has given us each a one-of-a-kind mix of qualities. We each have certain talent and potential, a particular energy level, tastes and affinities which make us different from anyone else. As we come to understand our distinctiveness, we are called to invest ourselves in the most effective possible way to help other people. Yet we are also obliged to be good stewards of the gift which God has made us to be. This means placing limits on ourselves—not for the sake of laziness or self-indulgence, but to be the best gift possible in our service for Christ.

As a friend of mine put it, "By declaring that he was fruitful in every good work, Paul certainly meant that he took on no more work than he could be fruitful in doing."

Respect Your Limits

Of course, life is never an exact science. Emergencies occur. We must always be willing to be flexible. At the same time we must not forget that we are part of a body of people. We can take our own importance too seriously and take on responsibility that would better be delegated.

Last fall a woman phoned me with an urgent request that I spend some sessions counseling her and her fiancé. While I try to bend to such needs whenever possible, it seemed to be one too many commitments for the period involved. If I granted her request, it would mean taking some evenings away from my children. The savior side of me wanted to respond and rescue her, and I almost agreed to meet with them. But I knew that this would keep me from being the gift I should be to my boys.

Suddenly I remembered a pastor-friend who had recently told me of his desire to begin a family counseling practice. I suggested that she phone him, and she was pleased with the idea. As it turned out, he was delighted to have this opportunity and probably did a better job helping them than I would have done. If I had given into my savior instinct, a number of people would have been less well served.

Each of us must learn to be the gift to others which God has designed us to be. While there is great responsibility in that calling, there is also great liberty, for we know that there are limits to our responsibility. As we work energetically within these limits, we will best serve others for Christ's sake.

21

Breaking
the Inertia

On a retreat this past fall I met two men who impressed me greatly. Each had taken a courageous step in finding his career niche. And each had increased the benefits in his professional life by, well, reducing them.

Alfred founded a printing business in his late teens, and it prospered. By age thirty-two he was financially secure and en route to becoming wealthy. Yet he felt that his most significant gifts were not being invested for Christ.

He carefully examined the options and concluded that his strongest talents and aspirations lay in health care. Yet he did not have the stamina for a vocation in general medicine or surgery. Nursing proved to be the viable alternative. Now, at age thirty-six, he has just graduated from nursing college and has begun serving in his first hospital position.

I was profoundly impressed with Alfred's enthusiasm for his work and the heartfelt dedication to his patients which he displayed. But what I admired most was his willingness to leave a high-paying profession and take four years off from life to prepare to take a new job at half his former salary. I must say I was impressed, too, with his willingness to enter a career which hasn't traditionally been considered a masculine one. He had taken bold steps to realize his potential for Christ.

The other man was Ray, a retiree who had spent most of his life working for the same large corporation. Yet at age forty he decided to leave a high-salaried, glamorous job for a less prestigious and far lower-paying position in the same company. He made the move for a simple reason: the new job better fit the skills and creative interests which he felt that God had given him. Now, nearly thirty years later, he has no regrets and still believes that the move was one of the most important of his life.

Exceptions to the Rule

These men stand out in my mind as inspiring exceptions to a pattern which plagues Americans today. Far too frequently our vocational choices are not really choices at all. We fall into vocations—more often from social convention than from an honest appraisal of our gifts and areas of motivation. And typically inertia or the desire for "upward mobility" keeps us locked into them.

When we look at the lives of great men and women of faith in Scripture, we see an almost consistent pattern of movement. Most of them came into the important adventures which God had for them only after they took certain bold strokes to break the inertia in their lives. For some the moves were geographical. Abraham left his homeland of Haran; Joseph, after being deported to Egypt, stayed there and did not attempt to return to Canaan; Naomi, when bereft of her husband and sons, left Moab for Bethlehem.

In other cases the moves were occupational. Moses, Saul, David, and others left the shepherding profession for positions of political and spiritual leadership. Some of Jesus' disciples left fishing vocations; at least one left a lucrative career in tax collecting; Joanna left a prestigious position in Herod's palace.

If these examples have anything to suggest to us today, they say that living the life of faith will usually require us to make some decisive moves to break out of stagnant patterns which have socked us in.

Changing the Default Modes

The most insidious inertia factor we have to contend with today is the lure of a fat paycheck. The problem is termed "golden hand-cuffs" in modern corporate life. This term refers to the squelching effect that promotions and salary raises can have on our personal potential. A person is pulled out of a position for which he is qualified and motivated and "upgraded" to a higher-paying, more prestigious position which doesn't tap his talents or interests nearly as well. With the benefit of a larger salary, though, he grows accustomed to a more extravagant lifestyle, and it becomes difficult to think of moving backward. He remains stuck in a job with good perks but minimal creative satisfaction.

I'm certainly not suggesting that we should have no concern with the financial rewards of our work. Scripture commands us to be involved in employment which provides our basic economic needs (2 Thess 3:6-10). Yet if we allow financial motives to be *primary* in choosing a profession, we're likely to doom ourselves to a life of wealthy mediocrity. The abundant life which Christ offers will never be realized until we're willing to compromise our lifestyle for the sake of better utilizing the gifts he's given us.

Geographical inertia is also a factor that hinders us today, in spite of the ease of transportation available to us. Nancy, a woman who came to me for vocational counseling, is a typical example. As a recent college graduate with a drama major, she was eager to find an opportunity to employ her acting skills in a Christian context. She asked if I knew of any professional drama ministries to which she might apply.

At the time, the only one I knew about was in Berkeley, California. I suggested that she fly there and audition. She quickly protested that she knew that God didn't want her going to Berkeley. It would be too far from family and friends. Finally she admitted that even if God clearly commanded her to move there, she wouldn't go. She was open to his will as long as it was within a half-hour radius of Washington, D.C.!

Many of us will find the best opportunities for employing our gifts only when we're willing to forge beyond our geographical comfort zone. I might add that doing so may also be a necessary step toward finding a life mate. If making such a move sounds like forcing the hand of God, I can only say that I think God expects us to take the same level of responsibility in seeking marriage as we do in looking for the best career opportunities. As we've noted, Ruth is a biblical example of someone who took such initiative.

The bottom line is that living the life of faith requires some movement. You and I need to be willing to break the inertia patterns that rob us of Christ's abundant life. The life of faith is meant to be a moving experience.

22

Trust Your
Judgment

Sometimes when counseling someone about a decision, I'll give this simple advice: *Trust your judgment.*

I may add something like: *You are in a better position to decide this matter than you realize. Make the choice that seems best to you, and believe that it is the right path to take. Yes, trust your judgment.*

There are two situations where I'm particularly inclined to offer this counsel. One is when someone has made a respectable effort to work through a decision yet cannot muster the courage to finally resolve it. A common example is a man (or woman) in a long-term relationship who cannot decide whether to go ahead with marriage. The relationship may be a solid, supportive one, and there may excellent reasons to choose to marry. The person may even be reasonably convinced that marriage is the right choice. Still, he hesitates, fearful that he isn't seeing things as clearly as he should. This is someone who needs to be strongly reassured of his ability to make a good decision.

Another person who needs this assurance is someone prone to value others' opinions above his or her own. This often is the case with the person who is fearful to break off a bad relationship. A woman, for example, is pursued by a man who makes every effort to win her affection. After giving it fair consideration, she concludes that the relationship wouldn't be right for her. Yet he persists, claiming that he has a better understanding of things than she does. He may even insist that he knows that God wills for them to be together. She wonders in all honesty if he is right. And since he is a stronger personality than she, it's easy to cave in to his persuasion. Again, my counsel to her is, "Trust your judgment."

Typically, this advice is greeted with some surprise. "Doesn't Scripture teach us *not* to trust our personal judgment?" people ask. "Doesn't Proverbs 3:5 tell us not to rely on our own understanding?"

I confess I wince a bit when I mete out this advice. Years of conditioning have left me with the same knee-jerk reaction to hearing "trust your judgment." It's typically taught in Christian circles that this is precisely what we *shouldn't* do. As the slogan of a popular seminar expresses it: *God's way: Exactly the opposite of my natural inclinations.* If we've been a Christian for any time, we've probably heard this notion preached so often that we feel irreverent even questioning it or considering whether there's another side to the story.

A Two-Sided Coin

Indeed, on one level Scripture does advise us to be skeptical about our own judgment. Proverbs 3:5-7 declares, "Trust in the LORD with all your heart and lean not on your own understanding; in all your ways acknowledge him, and he will make your paths straight. Do not be wise in your own eyes; fear the LORD and shun evil."

Yet the Proverbs also prod us to develop the ability to make wise decisions. Admonitions to seek wisdom permeate the Proverbs. While these are given to challenge us to grow in wisdom, they do show that gaining sound insight is a realizable goal. Consider Proverbs 3:13-14: "Blessed is the man who finds wisdom, the man who gains understanding, for she is more profitable than silver and yields better returns than gold." That statement and many like it throughout the Proverbs suggest that it's possible to exercise good judgment, at least if certain conditions are met.

Even more significant is Paul's assurance that we who follow Christ have "the mind of Christ" (1 Cor 2:16). This is a remarkable promise about the possibility of showing good judgment. Having the mind of Christ does not mean that our insights are infallible. Yet it does mean that we're beginning from an exceptional position of strength in our effort to make good decisions. As we make the right effort to clear our field of vision, we may be confident that we're seeing clearly to take steps of faith.

What do we need to do, then, to reach this point of confidence about our judgment? Here are several guidelines to keep in mind.

• *Question your first impressions.* We ought to have an inherent distrust of our first impressions. Ironically, it's those who find it possible to doubt their own judgment who are most capable of finally making competent decisions. But most often it's our *initial* assumptions which need to be called into question.

We have each been influenced far more than we realize by ideals of our secular and Christian cultures that hit wide of the mark of how God sees our lives. *Programmed* is a better word for it, for this influence strongly affects our standards of judgment. It's this internal programming which so often triggers our initial perceptions and renders them misleading.

Take "love at first sight," for instance. The romantic attraction that we first feel for someone—or the absence of it—often tells us little about our true compatibility with that person or our potential for a successful long-term relationship. In one survey 1,000 happily married individuals were asked whether, when they first met the one to whom they're now happily married, they believed this was the right person for them. A full 80 percent responded no. It took time for them to move beyond their initial impressions and appreciate the true potential of the other person—and the relationship.[1]

It's the same principle which writers, artists and other creative people almost always discover, sometimes the hard way. Writers often find that their first draft of a manuscript, no matter how lovingly nurtured, does not communicate effectively. A second or third revision makes all the difference. Artists have the same experience. Consider the testimony of Yasho Kumiyoshi:

I have often obtained in painting directly from the object that which appears to be the real results at the very first shot, but when that does happen, I purposely destroy what I have accomplished and redo it over and over again. In other words, that which comes easily I distrust. When I have condensed and simplified sufficiently I know then that I have something more than reality.[2]

Questioning our initial assumptions can be painful. Yet it's a critical beginning point in approaching any major decision. This, I'm convinced, is the concern underlying Proverbs 3:5-7. By urging us not to lean on our own understanding the writer is saying, "Don't be too quick to take your gut instincts and first impressions uncritically."

• *Get the facts.* We also need to make a reasonable effort to get the facts and weigh them carefully. This is the second condition for good judgment.

When we look at the many proverbs which stress the need for seeking wisdom, we find them pressing us to be diligent thinkers. They implore us to get pertinent information and prudently sift through it. "If you call out for insight and cry aloud for understanding, and if you look for it as for silver and search for it as for hidden treasure, then you will understand the fear of the LORD and find the knowledge of God" (Prov 2:3-5).

Our effort to gain insight in any important matter should not be halfhearted, the proverb stresses. We should seek the best information we can, consider it carefully and allow time for our insights to season. While the proverb clearly prompts us in this direction, it also assures us that we can be successful in this search. With the right effort, it promises, "you will find the knowledge of God"—or the *insight* of God. The verse that follows adds, "For the LORD gives wisdom, and from his mouth come knowledge and understanding."

This assurance that we can reach the point of judging wisely is vital to keep in mind, for it cautions us against endlessly analyzing a decision. While God calls us to be responsible decision-makers, he urges us to be good stewards of our time as well. The point comes when we should assume as a matter of faith that he has given us adequate insight to decide correctly. We should make a *reasonable* effort to get the facts and reflect on them. Then in faith we should trust that God has provided us enough information to make our decision.

Two people, for instance, who have dated seriously for two or three years, and have discussed the possibility of marriage for nearly this long, have usually gone well beyond making this reasonable effort. Typically they are at a saturation point of information. If you are in this position, the question to consider is whether by waiting longer you are likely to gain some radically new insight which will help your decision. If the answer is no, then you are at the point where a choice should be made. It makes sense now to trust your judgment—provided you are seeking the Lord's direction to begin with.

• *Pray for guidance.* This brings us to the third condition for good judgment—the need to pray for wisdom. Throughout the Proverbs we're told that wisdom and clear insight are a gift of God. In light of this, James 1:5 commands us, "If any of you lacks wisdom, he should ask God, who gives generously to all without finding fault, and it will be given to him."

Here again, though, the guiding word is *reasonable*. Make a *reasonable* effort to pray for insight. Remember that James promises that if we pray for wisdom, *it will be given.* Praying excessively for guidance may indicate that I don't believe that God is honoring his promise to provide it.

While many Christians don't take prayer seriously enough, some become obsessive about praying. It's striking that most of the significant prayers recorded in Scripture are *brief.* Even in Gethsemane, with the momentous events to follow, Jesus didn't command his disciples to pray endlessly but for "an hour" (Mt 26:40). This is liberating to consider, for it suggests that an hour may be a reasonable period to spend praying over a critical matter. Jesus was certainly not suggesting a rigid or legalistic time frame in telling his disciples pray for an hour, for the ancients did not have the precise time measurements we have today. Yet his advice does provide a general benchmark to follow in praying over a significant concern.

If you are facing a major decision—perhaps about a career change, a relationship or your involvement in your church—and have made a reasonable effort to get the facts and consider them, let me urge you now to give some attention to seeking God's direction. Set aside a period of uncluttered time—an hour, perhaps—and choose a quiet spot where you're not likely to be interrupted. Pray earnestly for God's insight. Ask him, too, for courage to step forward in faith as he directs you.

Then believe in faith that God is giving you the grace to think clearly. Trust your judgment. Go ahead and make your best choice. If in all honesty it seems that you still don't have enough information to decide, then don't force the decision. Choose to stay tentative—but make that definite choice with confidence.

But if there is reasonable evidence that you should move in a certain direction, then opt to do so, asking God to make it abundantly clear if you're not choosing the best course. Then move ahead confidently, even if some doubts remain. Look for *substantial* certainty but not perfect certainty

Beyond Mood Swings
If you're one who is indecisive or analytical by nature, realize that

there are some important benefits to your temperament. It gives you the energy and patience to carefully plod through all the angles of a decision. But realize the drawbacks it presents for you as well. You may be prone to overanalyze a decision or wait for a measure of "perfect peace" that isn't reasonable to expect before taking a major step.

Take confidence in knowing that if you are a child of Christ, God has given you the mind of Christ. He has put within you the capacity to make good judgments. Honor him by taking that ability seriously. And enjoy the incomparable adventure of decision-making.

VII

Confronting Our Fears of Change

23

When Better Seems Worse

In the days leading up to my ordination service, I was surprised to find that I dreaded the occasion as much as I looked forward to it. While I knew that important benefits would come from being ordained, the thought of taking the step frightened me. I feared that I didn't deserve the honor and wouldn't be able to handle the increased sense of significance it would bring.

Yet once the service was over and the formalities past—once there was no easy turning back—I suddenly felt at home with my new status. Never, in fact, during the twenty years since have I wavered in feeling comfortable with the distinction of being ordained, which in its own way has served to open many doors.

We may experience a multitude of fears when making a major personal change. We can fear success as much as failure, and—in relationships—commitment as much as rejection. So often, though, the heart of the problem is simply that *we don't like change*. When we look carefully at what frightens us, we find it is the fear of change that is holding us back.

This was clearly the case as I approached my ordination ceremony. Becoming ordained meant letting go of a comfortable old identity for an uncertain new one. And it meant growing up a bit, opening myself to new responsibilities. And that was scary.

Let's face it. Change of any sort—whether modest or major—can be unnerving to us. As journalist Ellen Goodman notes,

> We cling to even the minor routines with an odd tenacity. We're upset when the waitress who usually brings us coffee in the breakfast shop near the office suddenly quits, and are disoriented if the drugstore or the cleaner's in the neighborhood closes. ... We each have a litany of holiday rituals and everyday habits that we hold on to, and we often greet radical innovation with the enthusiasm of a baby meeting a new sitter.[1]

Of course we find unwelcome change unsettling. But this can be just as true when the change is one we strongly desire to make. That is to say, we can long for the change on one level yet fear it on another. Such ambivalence when making a major change is extremely common, although most people are surprised when they experience it. This vexing mixture of emotions is reflected by a comment in a recent news article on the trauma of changing your lifestyle: "Here I am, moving into a permanent relationship and we've just bought a wonderful new house. So why do I find selling my smaller condo so wrenching?"[2]

Not a few Christians are startled to experience such divided feelings after making a decision to marry. On at least eight occasions in the last year alone, Christians have sought my counsel due to cold feet after becoming engaged. One brilliant, mature Christian man went through three major episodes of doubt during the two months before his wedding, even though he had made the commitment to marry with great conviction of heart. In another case, a woman was ready to cancel her wedding on only ten days' notice. She had earnestly desired to marry this man and at the time of her engagement was certain that God was leading her to do so. Yet as their wedding day approached, her apprehensions grew to the point of practically overriding her better judgment.

As my ordination experience demonstrates, though, the fears we experience in the face of a major change are often deceptive. They are aggravated by our knowing that we still have the freedom to change our mind. Once we take the step and are no longer free to renege, they usually vanish. In the case of marriage, it typically happens that after the vows are taken and the festivities are over, the fears that were so disabling are forgotten.

We go through this identical process in other changes as well. Taking a decisive step is usually necessary to put our fears to rest.

Perfect Peace?

Complicating the matter for many Christians, though, is an unfortunate notion about Christ's peace. Many assume that if God is leading you to do something, you'll experience perfect peace. This is usually thought to mean that no fears or doubts will intrude: If you have any misgivings at all about taking the step, then God is warning you not to go ahead.

While Scripture teaches that Christ gives peace to those who follow him, it never guarantees that we will *feel* peaceful as we begin to take a step forward. God doesn't overrule our psyche. The peace that he gives, rather, enables us to *transcend* our fears—to move ahead in spite of many hesitations. We may feel a mixture of peace and fear at the same time, especially in the early stages of making a major change. Many of us are so constituted psychologically that we simply cannot feel peaceful *in advance* of a major step but only afterward. Taking the step is vital to experiencing Christ's peace and opening ourselves to the full blessings of God.

Indeed, faith often involves the resolve to move ahead in spite of fear.

The Lure of the Comfort Zone

The call of Moses provides a helpful example of these principles. When God confronted Moses through the burning bush, he offered

him an exceptional opportunity to do something meaningful with
his life. Yet Moses responded with extreme fear and reluctance:
"Who am I, that I should go to Pharaoh and bring the Israelites out
of Egypt? . . . 0 Lord, please send someone else to do it" (Ex 3:11;
4:13).

We could easily conclude that Moses didn't really want the
position that God was offering him. As a young man, though, he
had displayed exactly the aspirations which this position would now
fulfill. His passion to free his fellow Jews from oppression was so
great that it spurred him to murder an Egyptian whom he caught
abusing an Israelite (Ex 2:11-12). In all likelihood this zeal was
still inside of him, though it had been repressed for decades.

Fear of repercussions after he killed the Egyptian led Moses to
seek refuge in the desert. For forty years he worked as a shepherd
and lived in the home of a respected priest. We may guess that
while life was not bristling with adventure for Moses during this
time, it was not terribly stressful either. When God finally asked
Moses to deliver Israel, Moses expressed intense fears of failure.
Yet undoubtedly he feared change as well, for accepting the call
would mean leaving a number of familiar comforts.

Interestingly, as Moses responded to God's call, he not only
realized dramatic success but experienced remarkable fulfillment
too. Not that it was easy. He was stretched and challenged enor-
mously. Yet through the whole process came times of unparalleled
intimacy with God, substantial growth in his leadership skills, and
the radical joy of knowing that his life was accomplishing something noteworthy. We might add that his long-term physical vitality
probably benefited as well, for at the time of his death at the age of
one hundred twenty, "his eyes were not weak nor his strength gone"
(Deut 34:7).

Taking Control
Perhaps you are considering a major change. It may be a career
move or a new educational pursuit. Or a change in your living situ-

ation. Or a step forward in a relationship—or the breaking off of one. Or a change in your church affiliation, or a new venture in using your gifts within your church.

You may have approached this decision carefully and prayerfully and have good reason to believe that God is prompting you to go ahead. At the same time you're dogged with doubts and fears and a general uneasiness about making any change at all. If so, let me suggest five points of perspective to keep in mind:

1. Second thoughts are normal. No matter how mature you are spiritually and how diligently you have sought God's will, it is still common to have second thoughts about your decision. Yes, you may look with envy on friends who leap into marriage with perfect confidence that they have found God's choice, or on those who make career changes with surreal assurance that they're following God's will. Remember, though, that you are constructed differently psychologically than they are. You may even be a deeper thinker. And they may be ignoring misgivings which will come out later in more damaging ways. Be thankful that you recognize your feelings and don't repress them.

Remember, too, that Scripture is full of people, like Moses, who took major steps in the face of considerable ambivalence yet were clearly following God's will. Accept your psychological makeup for what it is.

2. Take time to mourn what you are leaving behind. No matter how greatly you desire to make this change, you're still letting go of certain cherished benefits in order to do it. The person eager for marriage, for instance, is relinquishing the treasured freedom of single life and forsaking forever the possibility of considering another option for an intimate relationship. Even when the change brings unquestioned improvements to your life, it's still normal to feel grief over what you're leaving behind. Don't be ashamed to face up to this. Take time to feel your grief and work through it. But don't let it hold you back from moving on to God's best.

3. Pray for strength and eagerness. While prayer has many

purposes in Scripture, one of the most essential is to gain courage when taking a major step of faith. Jesus gave us a vivid demonstration of this in Gethsemane. Through an hour or so of earnest prayer his outlook was transformed, and he gained the determination and confidence he needed to proceed with his mission. Give some dedicated time to praying about your decision. But don't merely ask for guidance—ask for strength and eagerness to take the course that is best for you. Praying in this fashion can make a significant difference.

4. Take control of your psyche. You have considerably more control than you probably realize over the mood swings which accompany a major personal change. The people with whom you associate, for instance, affect your outlook dramatically. There may be those who, regardless of their intentions, find it difficult to feel positive about the change you want to make. Their own identity is tied to how you are now. For you to change means adjustments for them too—in their routine, in their pattern of relating to you, in how they see themselves. They may not do anything overtly to discourage you from moving ahead. Still, it is difficult to be around them and not feel guilty for upsetting the equilibrium in their lives. You wonder if you should be making any change at all.

Others will be much more forward-looking in the way they see you. They are able to think beyond their own narrow concerns and appreciate what God is doing in your life. They trust your judgment and share your excitement for taking on new adventures and risks. And they genuinely want to see you succeed. They reflect the supremely supportive spirit which David displays in Psalm 20: "May [God] give you the desire of your heart and make all your plans succeed. We will shout for joy when you are victorious and will lift up our banners in the name of our God. May the LORD grant all your requests" (vv 4-5).

Don't forsake those who find it hard to agree with you. But give priority to spending time with those who are able to think creatively about your life. Their perspective will be contagious. Remember that Jesus himself chose to move away from Nazareth into settings where people's expectations of him were higher. This suggests that we should consider it a point of stewardship to avoid too much contact with negative people. We benefit most by being with those who see us dynamically.

5. Accept the principle of tradeoffs. In 1982, *Cosmopolitan* magazine editor Helen Gurley Brown published *Having It All.* The book became a bestseller and the title a byword for popular thinking in the 1980s. The having-it-all philosophy proclaims that through shrewd choices and careful management of our life we can enjoy all of the benefits that we seek. A near-perfect life is possible, if we will just take the right steps to bring it about.

The belief that we can have it all has subtly infected our outlook as Christians. Instead of expecting abundant life, we expect perfect life and assume that significant gain can come without pain.

While Scripture promises that Christ's blessings during this life are immense, it teaches that there are always tradeoffs involved in embracing them. Challenging choices must be made to let go of one benefit in order to enjoy another. Once we accept the reality of this—and that perfection is never possible in the choices we make—it becomes easier to take steps forward. Change itself becomes less threatening.

This point is so essential that we'll devote another chapter to it. First, though, it will help to look more carefully at the emotional challenge involved in revising our dreams.

24

Revising
the Map

A friend recently told me that he has let go of a major dream. Long ago his parents promised him they would one day move from their plush suburban home and allow him to purchase it at a nominal price. For nearly twenty years Nate looked forward to the day when he could move his family there. Though only a short distance from his current residence, it would be a big improvement in house and yard space and a much quieter neighborhood setting. And it would still provide easy access to his city job.

During the last year, though, Nate and his wife, Sherry, decided to consider a more radical change in lifestyle. They were attracted to a modest home for sale in the distant suburbs, which was close to recreational pursuits they enjoyed. They could reduce their living expenses by moving there, and with a smaller house to care for, they would have more time for other activities.

It seemed like the right move for them. But while they were weighing the possibility, Nate's parents announced that they were finally ready to move on to the next chapter in their lives. Nate could now buy their home. It was a wrenching decision for Nate and Sherry.

After much consideration they decided to tell Nate's parents no. While disappointing his folks was difficult enough, Nate confessed there was a greater challenge: "The hardest part was admitting *to myself* that I no longer wanted to do this."

Knowing my friend to be an unusually tenacious soul, I was impressed with his willingness to abandon a long-time desire in light of his new priorities. This showed remarkable maturity, for stubbornness could easily have kept him from changing course.

Nate's experience reminds us not only of the need for staying flexible as we plan our lives but of the challenge involved in doing so. Our goals and aspirations, no matter how well thought out, are always based upon limited information. Each day brings with it new insights and the need for changing our outlook at least slightly. From time to time our understanding has grown to the point where a major mid-course correction is indicated. Yet letting go of old ambitions can be the most difficult part of changing directions. Pride, stubbornness or the conviction that we must be true to ourselves can keep us bound to a dream that we've outgrown.

A critical part of maturing is learning to adjust our dreams to account for reality as we now know it. As I heard it aptly stated in a sermon recently, "Life is a continual process of revising the map."[1]

This is a principle which every successful person in business learns. An article in *Nation's Business* notes, "Almost without exception, the eventual performance of a prospective business will be influenced by external factors over which the business has little or no control."[2] Businesses which are able to adjust to changing market conditions survive and prosper. Those that insist on continuing to dispense a product or service which is no longer needed—or which is being more effectively provided by someone else—lose their edge and go under.

This same principle applies to relationships. We bring into friendships and fellowship experiences a "wish dream," as

Bonhoeffer terms it in *Life Together,* which can never be realized.[3] Finding meaningful friendships requires that we let go of our expectations of what others *should* be like and learn to love them as they are. The same is true with romance. Some adjusting of our image of the ideal partner is always needed if we are to find a suitable companion or build a healthy marriage.

Finding God's best for any area of our life always requires some revising of the map.

Locked in Concrete

As obvious as this principle may seem to be, it's one which Christians have a particularly hard time appreciating. Many carry an idea about God's guidance which makes it difficult to be flexible. They assume that when God guides us, he provides a revelation of our future. This notion is reflected in popular language used to speak of God's guidance: he provides a "call" to a vocation—suggesting an imperative laid on us for life. Or he gives us a "vision" for our life.

It's a small step from this idea to thinking that our dreams of the future are inspired by God and thus a mandate to be followed. To renege on them is to disobey God and show that we lack faith that he will bring them to pass. It's hard enough to rethink our life's direction without this perspective on God's guidance. With it, revising the map becomes even more difficult.

I remember a Christian couple who were convinced that God had revealed to them that they would come to own a certain house that was for sale, even though it was well beyond their financial limits. Even after it sold to someone else, they continued to assume that they would one day be the owners.

While some Christians insist on holding on to dreams beyond a reasonable point, others become disillusioned when their plans don't work out. A highly respected pastor told me that he was deeply frustrated over the failure of a radio ministry he had attempted to launch. "I carefully followed all the procedures for discerning God's will and am certain that the Lord led me to do this," he said. Yet he encountered unexpected problems and was compelled to abandon the project. He couldn't understand why it failed considering the clear guidance he had received. He felt that God and the Christian community had let him down.

Revision of Vision
One certainly cannot blame the Christian couple for setting their heart on what appeared to be their dream home. Nor can one fault the pastor for following what seemed to be God's will, then feeling disappointed when his efforts weren't successful. Yet both the couple and the pastor held a concept of God's guidance which set them up for disillusionment.

In truth, Scripture gives little support to the idea that God reveals our future when he guides us. Both the Old and New Testaments picture him as One who guides incrementally, in a step-by-step fashion. This is stated in beautifully symbolic language in Psalm 119:105: "Your word is a lamp to my feet and a light for my path." When you walk through the woods on a dark evening carrying a lantern or flashlight, the illumination is merely enough for taking the next step. Only after you take that step do you have light to take the one beyond. But that is all you need.

This suggests that reassessment will often be needed in finding God's will. This is a liberating perspective, for it will keep us from the presumption of the Christian couple who couldn't let go of their dream to own the home. It will also save us from the severe crisis of faith which the pastor experienced. I don't believe that the setbacks he encountered implied that he had misread God's will in beginning the radio ministry. They simply meant that reevaluation was now needed. God may have brought him to this point not to help him succeed in this particular endeavor but to give him enough light to understand a new and better direction to take from there.

This isn't to say that determination is unimportant in the Christian life. We should always move forward enthusiastically in view of the light that we have (Eph 5:17). Yet we shouldn't become unsettled when new insight suggests a change in direction. We should take heart, rather, that we are not locked in to an outmoded understanding of God's will but can move forward as he throws fresh light on our path.

25

Tradeoffs
Worth Making

I *spoke earlier about an experience of burnout which I had half-*way through a seminary program. I mentioned that talking with the dean of students made all the difference. Through his counsel I gained the zeal to tackle my studies again.

The essence of his advice was simple: I needed to be willing to make some tradeoffs. It was a reasonable tradeoff, he said, to spend some dry time in exchange for the creative period that I'd already enjoyed. Besides, I would soon finish the program and could then begin to enjoy its benefits. When all of the angles were considered, the tradeoffs were certainly more than worth it.

As basic as this advice was, it hit a receptive chord with me. It was the right thought at the right time and gave me fresh heart. Once it dawned on me that it was okay to make some tradeoffs in order to complete the program, I felt comfortable doing so.

The concept of making tradeoffs has stuck with me and often been the redemptive thought helping me over the hump in difficult decisions. Not that getting beyond the hump is always easy. As a perfectionist, I approach what I do idealistically. I think in terms of maximizing my potential. Yet I always find that tradeoffs are needed in any significant step that I take. Initially, facing the need for them is a jolt to my idealism—a blow to the lie I've absorbed from my culture that I can "have it all." As it gradually sinks in that these tradeoffs are not only normal but desirable, they become easier to accept.

We instinctively resist the notion of making tradeoffs, for it smacks of compromising. We fear "settling"—to quote the term so often used today by those considering an opportunity for marriage. We dread the thought of selling short our ideals or acquiescing to less than God's best for our life. As necessary as these fears are, we must be careful that they don't dissuade us from tradeoffs which are actually healthy and beneficial to make. Yes, following God's will should never entail compromising. It should never involve settling. Yet it often does require letting go of an unreasonable ideal for the sake of a reasonable one.

Or a lesser ideal for the sake of a better one.

Or an ideal which no longer fits us well for one that now better applies.

Such exchanges of ideals are essential if we are to realize our potential for Christ and experience the fulfillment he offers. They are almost always needed in decisions for marriage, parenting, career, and other major steps as well. They are at the heart of what it means to make choices which reflect God's best for us.

Tradeoffs in St. Paul's Life

St. Paul was familiar with the need for making tradeoffs. In Philippians 1, for instance, he speaks of his desire to die and be with Christ. Far from having a suicidal urge, Paul simply recognized that the blessedness of living in eternity with Christ would be unparalleled by any pleasure that he enjoyed on earth. At the same time, he saw advantages to his homecoming being delayed. Staying on earth would allow him to invest his life in other people—to win some to Christ, and to disciple as many Christians as possible. "If I am to go on living in the body, this will mean fruitful labor for me. . . . I desire to depart and be with Christ, which is better by far; but it is more necessary for you that I remain in the body. Convinced of this, . . . I will remain . . . for your progress and joy in the faith" (Phil 1:22-25).

This same capacity to think in terms of tradeoffs even allowed him to experience considerable joy while in prison, for he realized the remarkable way God was using his internment to influence others. Not only was he having exceptional opportunities to tell members of the palace guard about Christ, but many Christians were gaining courage from Paul's example to share their faith in challenging circumstances (Phil 1:12-14).

Getting Specific

Let's look at some common ways that the need for making tradeoffs applies in our Christian walk today. While this list is anything but exhaustive, it includes some perspectives which are especially helpful to keep in mind when considering a major change in our life's direction.

1. Trading affirmation for creative accomplishment. We spend much of our energy trying to win the approval of other people. The desire to be liked, accepted and acclaimed by others is one of our central motives. For some it's the primary basis for everything they do.

This has its positive side. It spurs us to move outside of ourselves, to seek relationships and live a life which has value to others. It also opens us to being influenced by other people. Others sometimes see our potential better than we do. Their encouragement helps us find the resolve to realize our potential and to take important steps of growth.

But our desire for affirmation also has its negative side. We cannot please everyone. And invariably there are those—sometimes close friends or family members—who think of us statically and don't wish to see us change. They feel threatened if we grow, fearing that a piece of their own identity will be lost in the process. Their influence is deadening to our motivation, for we fear hurting them or losing their affection if we move forward.

Fortunately God has so constructed our psyche that we find fulfillment not only in pleasing others but in creative accomplishment as well. This fact doesn't jump out and strike us as quickly as the more obvious fact that it feels good to be affirmed. Yet when we have the privilege of completing a project or making meaningful progress toward a goal, we're often surprised at how strong our sense of satisfaction actually is.

Which is to say that it's a reasonable tradeoff to purposely decide to let go of some affirmation in order to be more effective in areas where God has gifted us creatively. Of course I'm not suggesting that you commit social suicide in the process. Telling others where they can get off is not the point. You will not benefit by snubbing nonsupportive friends and risking the loss of their affection. Yet if you lose *some* affirmation in the process of developing your potential or moving toward a goal, that's okay. Your overall experience off fulfillment will likely not diminish but increase.

And you'll undoubtedly gain new friends in the process, who will appreciate you in your new role and affirm you in it.

2. Trading financial gain or lifestyle benefits for creative accomplishment. A related point is that it's worth letting go of material benefits in order to increase our creative satisfaction in the work we do. As we noted earlier, this is not a natural adjustment to make. The underlying current in American society is that your personal worth is measured by the size of your salary, the type of car you drive and the neighborhood in which you live. And of course the implication is that as these factors improve, your happiness will increase as well.

Whatever pleasure comes from economic benefits, though, pales in the face of the joy of using our most significant gifts and doing work which we're truly motivated to do. Still, as one psychiatrist observes, "It is extremely unusual in this society to make purposeful decisions to make less money."[1] This can be one of the most challenging and courageous steps we ever take.

Again, the tradeoff can be worth it, if in return you gain the opportunity to do work which better reflects your gifts and creative interests. While providing for your basic economic needs is essential (2 Thess 3:6-10), don't let this goal become all-encompassing. If you have the responsibility to provide for a family, remember that part of caring for family members is *encouraging* them. Since you can best encourage others when you're encouraged yourself, your work satisfaction will make a difference in your ability to love those in your family. This consideration should be weighed carefully along with financial benefits in thinking through any job option.

3. Trading professional activity for family life. This brings us to another tradeoff which has critical implications for those of us who are married. While it is wonderful to be involved in work that is creatively stimulating, we can become obsessed with work to the point that our family life suffers. When this happens, the quality of our work often deteriorates as well.

Canadian physician and stress expert Peter Hanson notes that poor family relationships contribute more to unhealthy stress than any other factor in our lives.[2] Tension within the family easily robs us of the creative energy we need for carrying out our professional work and other responsibilities. The converse is also true: good family relationships are a tonic inspiring creative energy and freeing us to be productive in what we do.

For people who are not married, the same holds true: the meaningful relationships in your life, whether with relatives or friends, and particularly with the "family" that makes up your household, must not get crowded out by job or other responsibilities. Both the people close to you and you yourself need and deserve prime time and attention.

Time spent building my relationships with those closest to me

doesn't have to be a distraction from realizing my professional aspirations. Indeed, it can be the most important investment I make
toward those goals. The key is to strike a healthy balance here.

   4. *Trading immediate pleasure or accomplishment for personal
growth.* Because we take pleasure from the experience of personal
growth, sacrificing immediate gains for the sake of long-term growth
is very often worth the exchange. This is a vital point to remember
when weighing educational opportunities vs. immediate options for
employment, for instance.

   We remember that our Lord himself spent thirty years of preparation for a ministry that lasted only three. Paul, too, after his dramatic call on Damascus Road, retreated for a fourteen-year
preparation period.

   Billy Graham reminisced at an evangelism workshop that if he
had his life to live over, he would preach less and study more. He
also remarked that if he knew he had but three years to live, he
would study two and preach only one.

   The personal growth tradeoff is one of the most helpful consid-
erations to keep in mind in a marriage decision. Unfortunately it is
usually the most overlooked. I was counseling an engaged woman
recently who was having second thoughts about going ahead with
her marriage. For Lisa, the concern was whether her fiancé would
be able to meet all of her needs and live up to all of her ideals. I
suggested that she give as much consideration to how he would
help her grow as she did to whether he would *make her happy.*

   Each of us who is thinking about marriage will do well to keep
this consideration in the forefront of our mind. I'm certain that God
gives us marriage at least as much for the sake of our development
as for our fulfillment. We're talking about a fifty-fifty proposition
here. While he uses marriage to meet our needs for companionship,
he also uses it to challenge us to grow into a more compassionate,
sensitive individual, by placing us in a lifetime relationship with
someone who is far short of perfect. Understanding this dynamic
can simplify a marriage decision, in some cases considerably. It

also can do wonders to help us value our spouse once we're married—especially at times when it seems that he or she is not living up to our image of the ideal mate.

5. *Trading ecstasy for the comfort of a secure, supportive relationship.* On vacation this past summer I read Christian psychologist André Bustanoby's insightful book *Can Men and Women Be Just Friends?* Bustanoby laments how many leave a good, comfortable marriage in search of a new attraction. They long for a relationship as electrifying as the one with their spouse once was. They fall for someone new, all the moonstruck sensations are there, and so they marry again. Within a year, though, the romantic feelings have mellowed and the relationship now seems, well, ordinary.

In a long-term relationship, Bustanoby explains, it is psychologically impossible to maintain the extreme romantic elation often present in the early days of getting acquainted. The initial exhilaration in romance—termed "temporary insanity" by another writer—is sparked by newness and mystery in the relationship, which by definition cannot last indefinitely. But in its place can come a quality of friendship which over the years continues to grow and offers extraordinary support and security. Bustanoby argues that it's well worth letting go of some ecstasy for the sake of this more stable benefit.[3]

This perspective is a redemptive one and, frankly, indispensable for a successful marriage relationship. It's an important outlook to keep in mind in choosing a marriage partner, too, for usually we place too much weight on romantic feelings. In the long run it's our friendship with the other that provides the most enduring—and satisfying—basis for marriage.

Looking beyond marriage to our other relationships, here too the exhilaration of a new friendship with a person who seems to have much to offer us can lure us away from more mundane but lasting friendships we already have. It's important to nourish our ongoing friendships and not drop them in favor of a new one which may or may not last. We must always beware of *using* people.

6. *Trading security for adventure.* At the same time, God does wish to bring a definite measure of adventure into our lives. The desire for new experiences is recognized by psychologists as a basic human need. *Contrast* is essential to our vitality. While this must not be the basis for leaving a comfortable marriage for a supposedly more enticing relationship, it's often a good reason for making career or lifestyle changes. The tragedy is that as we grow older and become more comfortable, we easily lose our willingness to risk. We place security above adventure.

In his classic *The Adventure of Living* Paul Tournier points out that we have an inherent need for adventure and stresses that this is a God-given instinct.[4] I agree heartily with his emphasis and recommend this book as the best treatment I have seen of the role of adventure in human life. We each need a certain balance between security and adventure. It's good from time to time to take inventory to make certain that the scales haven't tipped too greatly in one direction or the other.

7. *Trading activity for time with Christ.* Finally, I cannot speak of tradeoffs in the Christian life without saying something about our need for scheduling regular devotional time with Christ. Most of us are busy enough that a regular quiet time simply can't happen unless we're willing to put some other things aside. For many of us it means cutting back on our professional work or curtailing our other goals a bit. Here the greatest test to our faith often comes, for we prove whether we really believe that time with Christ is worth the sacrifice elsewhere.

Again, must I say it? The tradeoff is much more than worth it. Regular time spent with Christ benefits us in a multitude of ways— giving us increased vitality in what we do, building in us greater confidence of his presence and guidance, and opening us more fully to his work and provision in our lives.

26

The Greatness of Small Beginnings

Letting go of the past is one of the greatest challenges we face. In any major personal change, no matter how greatly we desire the benefits that the change will bring, we still have to come to terms with what we're leaving behind.

Learning to think in terms of revising the map and making tradeoffs can help considerably. But even as we become comfortable with the idea of taking a new direction, there is still plenty of inertia to overcome. Unless we believe that we can be successful in what we're undertaking, we're not likely to find the motivation to move ahead. Throughout this book we've considered perspectives which can help us identify reasonable hopes for success.

Still, getting started is often the most difficult thing we have to do. There is no momentum yet to spur us on and no feedback to encourage us. Taking the first step up the mountain, too, can seem hopeless in light of how high the summit actually is. It's here that our perspective on what it means to walk in faith needs to grow and expand. It helps to have a special understanding of the dynamics involved in taking the first steps toward a goal. While there are special challenges involved in this initial effort, considerable benefits come along with them. To say that we may experience a special measure of grace at this time is not stretching things too much.

We need, in short, a greater esteem for the small beginnings in life. "Don't despise the day of small beginnings," as Pat Robertson is fond of paraphrasing Zechariah 4:10. This is clearly an area which deserves our closest attention.

The Benefit of Hindsight

It is usually easiest to appreciate the value of the small beginning when we reflect on our past experience. Consider for a moment dreams or goals you've had which have been realized. Think back on those accomplishments or successful experiences which are most meaningful to you. I'm willing to guess that more than one of them had a rather tentative, inglorious start.

When we look carefully at the path which led to a personal success, we often realize that it began with a modest step forward which in time reaped a much greater harvest than we anticipated.

Such small first steps might include the following:

• An awkward first visit to a church singles group, which led to meeting the person you married.

• A hesitant phone call to ask someone out, or to inquire about a job opportunity, which received a much more positive response than you expected.

• A letter of application for a grant, written with a sense of futility, thinking you'd probably be better off spending your time doing something else. Yet to your astonishment the grant was given, and significant doors have now opened through that one effort.

• A business venture, begun with a paltry investment, which succeeded far beyond your expectations.

• A book, picked up in a time of discouragement, that inspired you and gave you the perspective to pursue your dream.

• A reconciled relationship, now going strong, which began with a simple request for forgiveness.

With the eyes of hindsight, we look back to such starting efforts with awe and gratitude. We realize there was greatness in that moment of small beginning which we didn't begin to appreciate at the time. We may shudder, too, to think of how close we came to not taking that one initial step which opened such important doors.

From Little Acorns . . .

Unfortunately the benefit of the small beginning is often lost on us when we face the possibility of embarking on new dream. The effort it would take to pursue it seems massive; we're overwhelmed with the impossibility of it all. There seems to be little or nothing we can do to move forward.

To the eyes of faith, though, there is a world of difference between "little" and "nothing." Often there is *something* we can do— some obvious first step we can take. This may be exactly what is needed to put the wheels of faith in motion.

For one thing, we shouldn't underestimate the value that taking any initial step toward a goal has upon us psychologically. Suddenly our psyche is committed, and we become more alert to opportunities which will move us toward our dream. Other people become more aware of our intentions as well and are more likely to try to help us.

Yet the spiritual aspect of taking the first step is even more important. The seemingly insignificant small beginning often gets much closer to the heart of the biblical idea of going forward in faith than we realize.

We don't usually think of it this way. The very notion of moving out in faith seems to imply taking a bold, extravagant step of some sort. We quickly think of the biblical prototypes: Moses parting the Red Sea, Joshua leading the Israelites to demolish the wall of Jericho with a shout, David marshaling his troops for battle, Gideon confronting the indomitable Midianite army with only three hundred soldiers, Esther going before King Ahasuerus knowing that her life hung in the balance, Peter preaching salvation to the large throng of Jews gathered on the day of Pentecost. It's easy to conclude that if we're not throwing caution to the winds, we're not really taking a step of faith.

Yet Scripture also shows great respect for the small, subtle, unspectacular first step. Consider these examples:

• In the parable of the talents Jesus commended the two servants who invested their money and upbraided the one who failed to give his one coin to the bankers (Mt 25:14-30). Few first steps are less inspiring than putting money in the bank. No one notices, there are no neon lights, and there is no immediate reward for this act of discipline. In fact, the period you must wait for any significant benefit can seem interminable. Yet with time the incremental gains grow larger and larger and the eventual profit is considerable.

It is striking that Jesus paid such respect to prudent financial investment. Clearly, too, he intended the parable of the talents to be an analogy to other areas of life where we take risks for his sake. It conveys an unmistakable lesson—that we shouldn't neglect the benefit of a small beginning in any venture of faith.

• One of the most celebrated marriages in Scripture resulted from a small, ignoble step forward. Ruth's marriage to Boaz came about because she and Naomi moved from Moab to Bethlehem. As we've noted, the move was anything but a triumphant one for these two women. During the ten years that Naomi lived in Moab, her husband and both sons—one married to Ruth —died. Naomi and Ruth, then, traveled to Bethlehem as widows. Naomi decided to make the move because famine no longer ravaged her homeland; undoubtedly, too, she hoped to find support from friends and family who still lived there. Ruth accompanied Naomi out of devotion to her mother-in-law. While they each obviously expected some benefits to come from this move, it's clear that neither expected a major improvement. Naomi's attitude upon returning home, in fact, can best be described as grief-stricken. The move was more one of necessity than of vibrant vision for the future.

Yet at least they did *something* to break the inertia of their grief and make a fresh start. In time the move brought blessings which surely exceeded their wildest expectations. It opened the opportunity for Ruth to meet and marry Boaz, then to give birth to a boy who was an ancestor of David. The new family connections brought healing and purpose not only to Ruth but also to Naomi, who felt that God had given her a new lease on life. An unglamorous step forward opened a wellspring of life for Naomi, Ruth, Boaz and countless others who benefited from the family relationships which resulted in generations that followed—including the birth of the Messiah.

• Nehemiah is one of the great heroes of Scripture. When we think of this Old Testament saint, we remember how, against all odds, he mobilized the remnant of Israel to rebuild the wall of Jerusalem, then reestablished the city as the center of Jewish worship life. As spectacular as this undertaking was, it began with a quiet, unspectacular step by Nehemiah which no one else knew he had taken. He made an earnest prayer, asking God to bring about the restoration of Jerusalem and committing himself to obedience in the matter (Neh 1:5-11).

As the book of Nehemiah unfolds, it becomes clear that Nehemiah's prayer had several far-reaching results. For one, God answered the details of his prayer resoundingly, bringing speedy and triumphant success to the reconstruction effort. Yet through the process of expressing his concerns to God, Nehemiah himself became emotionally committed to the goal of restoring Jerusalem. Shortly after making the prayer, Nehemiah, who was the royal cupbearer, served wine to the king, not intending to share his concern about Jerusalem with him. The king, however, discerned from Nehemiah's countenance that something was troubling him and asked him about it. Since Nehemiah was now personally committed to Jerusalem's revival, he was able to seize the moment. He not only told the king of the need but made a specific request for assistance, which the king granted (Neh 2:1-9).

Nehemiah's example is one of the most helpful we find in Scripture of the effect that merely committing ourselves internally to a goal can have upon our reaching it. It demonstrates with equal force how a determined, heartfelt prayer can serve to inaugurate a goal. His example inspires us to see these private steps as crucial beginnings toward any purpose we wish to accomplish. Simply by setting our heart toward pursuing a dream and committing our concern sincerely to God, we are beginning from a position of strength.

• We tend to glamorize the healing incidents in the Gospels and assume that those who came to Jesus for help did so boldly, with sublime confidence that they would be instantly cured. I'm certain, though, that many came in the same ambivalent, tentative spirit in which we often seek medical help today. The woman with the hemorrhage is a case in point, as we noted earlier. Terribly concerned that no one would notice her, and uncertain whether approaching Jesus was even appropriate, she decided merely to touch the hem of his garment. That one small gesture brought not only her healing but an effusive compliment from Jesus about her faith.

As we see here, Scripture describes small first steps which reaped a surprising harvest immediately, as well as those which brought results over time. Virtually all of the healing miracles mentioned in Scripture fit this pattern of immediate blessing. The "miracles of expansion" do as well. These include incidents in the Old and New Testaments where large crowds were fed with a small provision of food (2 Kings 4:42-44; Mk 6:33-44; 8:1-9) and the miraculous provision of oil which saved the prophet's widow from financial ruin (2 Kings 4:1-7). While we cannot presume that our own small first steps will immediately produce such astonishing results, we can never know unless we try.

And in time the results of a meager first effort often do surprise us.

The Challenge of Small Beginnings

While taking the small first step can make all the difference, there are two factors which can keep us from appreciating the special opportunity that we have for moving forward. One is that because of its apparent insignificance, we may not even recognize the small beginning that is possible for us to make. This was the case with Jesus' anxious, hungry disciples who didn't notice the loaf of bread they had in the boat with them. "They discussed this with one another and said, 'It is because we have no bread'" (Mk 8:16).

Elijah's experience of burnout is another case in point (1 Kings 19:1-8). Severely fatigued from a successful but exhausting confrontation with four hundred prophets of Baal, Elijah is thrown into a frenzy by a death threat from Queen Jezebel. I doubt that Jezebel could have found anyone willing to murder Eljjah at this time, considering the renown he had gained from his encounter with the Baal prophets. Otherwise, she would not have given Elijah the benefit of a warning which could allow him to escape. As it was, the best she could do was send him a taunting message. I'm certain that in a more coherent state Elijah would have recognized the implausibility of Jezebel's threat. Yet his apprehensions grew so out of hand that he fled to the desert for safety, abandoning his servant on the way. At this point his overwhelming anxiety, and his remorse over acting cowardly, led him to conclude that only a spectacular step could end his agony: suicide. He asked God to take his life.

In reality a much simpler step was needed to restore Elijah's emotional balance: food and rest. Fortunately God intervened, providing peaceful sleep and physical sustenance for the prophet. After two days of refreshing rest and relaxation his motivation returned. Yet left to his own resources, Elijah would have missed this small beginning which saved both his life and ministry.

Like the disciples in the boat or Elijah at his point of exhaustion, you and I can miss the small step that is available to us. A woman whom I know, Nancy, recently left a well-paying nursing job to enter a doctoral program. Though she had long desired to pursue this goal, she assumed it was financially impossible, being a single parent in her forties. Finally Nancy faced up to the fact that there was a small beginning she could make, which was to apply for grants. She made six applications, assuming her prospects for success were minimal. To her astonishment, four of the six were granted. When Nancy shared this personal triumph with me, I couldn't help but think of how many people there must be who need this same financial assistance—and would qualify for it—yet have concluded that it isn't worth the trouble to apply. Nancy herself overlooked this option for years.

Of course, writing a grant application means some uninspiring paperwork, and this suggests a second factor which can keep us from recognizing the chance to make a small beginning—the fact that we may look with contempt upon what we have to do.

Such was the near-fatal flaw of Naaman the leper in the Old Testament. Naaman sought healing for leprosy from Elisha, who told him to wash seven times in the Jordan River. Naaman's response was one of anger: "I thought that he would surely come out to me and stand and call on the name of the LORD his God, wave his hand over the spot and cure me of my leprosy. Are not Abana and Pharpar, the rivers of Damascus, better than any of the waters of Israel? Couldn't I wash in them and be cleansed?" (2 Kings 5:11-12). The text concludes, "He turned and went off in a rage."

Naaman's servants had the good sense to challenge him, saying, "If the prophet had told you to do some great thing, would you not have done it? How much more, then, when he tells you, 'Wash and be cleansed'!" (v. 13). Naaman fortunately repented of his obstinacy and followed the prophet's counsel. Yet his example warns us that no matter how greatly we want to reach a goal, our disdain for some of the details may keep us from moving forward. The initial steps that we must take are particularly likely to seem distasteful to us.

Pat Robertson is right in suggesting that our natural inclination is to despise the small beginnings of life. We need to make a conscious effort to counteract this tendency. We should remind ourselves often that we have considerable reason to esteem the small beginning, to celebrate it and be hopeful that in time our fledgling effort will bear significant fruit.

Taking Heart

Do you have a personal dream which has not been realized? To the best of your knowledge, is your dream in line with God's best intentions for your life? Yet does it seem that there is little or nothing you can do to move toward your goal—that your hands are tied?

Remember that a small beginning is sometimes the very step needed to open yourself to the provision of Christ. Remember that God's hand in your life is not shortened. Pray earnestly and look honestly at what you actually can do to start moving toward your goal. Don't look with contempt on the small beginning. Think of it as the launching point for a journey of optimistic faith.

Notes

Chapter 1: A Well-Founded Choice
[1]Richard Nelson Bolles, *What Color Is Your Parachute? A Practical Manual for Job Hunters and Career-Changers* (Berkeley Calif.: Ten Speed Press, revised annually).

Chapter 4: Serving Christ for the (Highest) Benefits
[1]Daniel P. Fuller, *The Unity of the Bible* (Grand Rapids, Mich.: Zondervan, 1993), pp. 151, 263-64, 352.
[2]C. S. Lewis, *The Weight of Glory and Other Addresses* (New York: Macmillan, 1949), pp. 1-2.

Chapter 6: When Is a Door Really Closed?
[1]Garry Friesen with J. Robin Maxson, *Decision Making and the Will of God: A Biblical Alternative to the Traditional View* (Portland, Ore.: Multnomah, 1980), p. 221.

Chapter 8: Self-Talk: How Much Can We Psych Ourselves Up?
[1]Shad Helmstetter, *The Self-Talk Solution: Take Control of Your Life—With the Self-Management Program for Success!* (New York: Pocket Books, 1988).

Chapter 9: Contagious Optimism
[1]Paul Tournier, *The Person Reborn* (New York: Harper & Row, 1966), pp. 139-73.

Chapter 10: A Matter of Timing
[1]Kenneth Scott Latourette, *A History of Christianity* (New York: Harper & Row, 1953), p. 21.

Chapter 12: Rumors of Miracles
[1]M. Scott Peck, *The Road Less Traveled: A New Psychology of Love, Traditional Values and Spiritual Growth* (New York: Touchstone Books, 1978); see especially pp. 253-60.
[2]Leon Morris, *The Gospel According to John*, New International Commentary (Grand Rapids, Mich.: Eerdmans, 1971), pp. 478-79.

Chapter 13: The Availability Factor
[1]Andrew Murray, *With Christ in the School of Prayer* (Old Tappan, N.J.: Revel, 1974), p. 103.

Chapter 16: Winning Through Failure
[1]Paul Tournier, *The Adventure of Living* (New York: Harper & Row, 1965), p. 127.
[2]Thomas J. Peters and Robert H. Waterman Jr., *In Search of Excellence: Lessons from America's Best-Run Companies* (New York: Warner Books, 1982), pp. 223-24, 286.

Chapter 17: It's Okay Not to Feel OK
[1]Lesley Hazelton, *The Right to Feel Bad: Coming to Terms with Normal Depression* (New York: Dial Press, 1984), pp. 42-43.
[2]Walter Trobisch, *Love Yourself* (Downers Grove, Ill.: InterVarsity Press, 1976), p. 50.

Chapter 22: Trust Your Judgment
[1]Nita Tucker with Debra Feinstein, *Beyond Cinderella: How to Find*

and Marry the Man You Want (New York: St. Martin's Press, 1987), p. 57.

[2]Brewster Ghiselin, ed., *The Creative Process* (New York: Mentor Books, 1952), p. 61.

Chapter 23: When Better Seems Worse

[1]Ellen Goodman, *Turning Points* (New York: Fawcett Crest, 1979), p. 15.

[2]Susan Porter Robinson, "In a Period of Transition," *The Washington Post,* March 22, 1990, Style section.

Chapter 24: Revising the Map

[1]Preached by Robert C. Crowley, pastor of Montrose Baptist Church, Rockville, Maryland.

[2]"The Arthur Young Business Plan Guide," *Nation's Business,* July 1987, p. 16.

[3]Dietrich Bonhoeffer, *Life Together,* trans. John W. Doberstein (New York: Harper & Brothers, 1954), pp. 26-30.

Chapter 25: Tradeoffs Worth Making

[1]Goodman, *Turning Points,* p. 30.

[2]Peter G. Hanson, *The Joy of Stress* (Kansas City, Mo.: Andrews, McMeel and Parker, 1985), pp. 45-46, 72-73, 104-5.

[3]André Bustanoby, *Can Men and Women Be Just Friends?* (Grand Rapids, Mich.: Pyranee Books, 1985), pp. 116-19.

[4]Tournier, *The Adventure of Living.*

About the Author

Blaine Smith, a Presbyterian pastor, spent 30 years as director of Nehemiah Ministries, Inc., a resource ministry based in the Washington, D.C. area. He retired the organization in 2009, but continues to use the name Nehemiah Ministries for free-lance work.

His career has included giving seminars and lectures, speaking at conferences, counseling, and writing. He is author of nine books, including *Knowing God's Will* (original and revised editions), *Should I Get Married?* (original and revised editions), *The Yes Anxiety*, *Overcoming Shyness*, *Faith and Optimism: Positive Expecation in the Christian Life* (originally *The Optimism Factor*), *One of a Kind*, and *Marry a Friend*, as well as numerous articles (all books except *Marry a Friend* published by InterVarsity Press, though several are now republished by SilverCrest Books). These books have been published in more than thirty English language and international editions. He is also lecturer for *Guidance By The Book*, a home study course with audio cassettes produced by the Christian Broadcasting Network as part of their *Living By The Book* series.

Blaine served previously as founder/director of the Sons of Thunder, believed by many to be America's first active Christian rock band, and as assistant pastor of Memorial Presbyterian Church in St. Louis. He is an avid guitarist, and currently performs with the Newports, an oldies band active in the Washington, D.C. area.

Blaine is a graduate of Georgetown University, and also holds a Master of Divinity from Wesley Theological Seminary and a Doctor of Ministry from Fuller Theological Seminary. He and Evie live in Gaithersburg, Maryland. They've been married since 1973, and have two grown sons, Benjamin and Nathan. Their first grandchild, Jackson Olen, was born to Ben and his wife Lorinda in 2009.

Blaine also authors a twice-monthly online newsletter, *Nehemiah Notes*, featuring a practical article on the Christian faith, posted on his ministry website and available by e-mail for free. You may e-mail Blaine at mbs@nehemiahministries.com.